Unexpected Blessings

Lyndia McMillan

Lyndia McMillan

CROSSBOOKS
PUBLISHING

CrossBooks™
A Division of LifeWay
1663 Liberty Drive
Bloomington, IN 47403
www.crossbooks.com
Phone: 1-866-879-0502

First published by CrossBooks 05/20/2011

ISBN: 978-1-6150-7880-6 (sc)
ISBN: 978-1-6150-7881-3 (hc)

Printed in the United States of America
This book is printed on acid-free paper.

Contents

Acknowledgments   vii
Foreword   ix

My Journey Of Faith   1
From Lyndia's Journal   11
Our Story   37
Don's Hospitalization And Home-Going   57
Scriptures   69
Grief Intermingled With Joy   73
The Journal Of Donald David Mcmillan   81
Receive God's gift of Salvation and Eternal Life   97

Acknowledgments

The Lord has enriched my life greatly by blessing me with wonderful Christian sisters and brothers in Christ. They were avid prayer warriors throughout Don's illness, through his home-going, and they continue to pray for me as I process the grief. There were many calls, encouraging notes, and numerous cards for which there are not enough words to convey my thankfulness and gratitude.

Don's family is my family, another incredible blessing! They continue to include and surround me, treating me as their own. God's love abounds!

Catherine Jones has spent many hours helping me write and rearrange the words of this book that they might make better sense to its readers. Saying thank you hardly seems enough. Her prayers and encouragement have been invaluable, her friendship a much treasured gift. Thank you for walking with me Catherine, my much cherished friend.

I am blessed to be a part of a small prayer group, an integral part of my life. They have also been faithful to pray for me and encourage me.

With all my heart, I praise and thank my heavenly Father who has brought me through every day and night, through the days of uncertainty and suffering, through the nights of aloneness and grief. Oh, that I would continue to be transformed into His image, made a reflection of Christ's glory to others, and growing in my love relationship with Him. Blessed be the name of the Lord! He is greatly to be praised!

Foreword

"Come here, Catherine. You have got to see this!"

Unsure of what had captured my pastor's attention I rose from my chair and moved towards the large window which looked out onto the street below us.

"Aren't they sweet, so in love?"

Locking onto the two figures that had him so transfixed, I had to agree with Pastor Sawyer, "they" certainly were adorable. Tightly clasping one another's hands, they swung their arms back and forth much as the pendulum in a fast clock. Our church's most recent newlyweds seemed to skip from the nearby parking lot all the way into the church office. Suddenly my thoughts shifted into reverse, and I was taken back to the time just a few months earlier when I had shared a hotel room with the bride, only she wasn't a bride at the time.

Lyndia (then Lyndia Taylor) and I had gone out of state to attend a Christian conference, and after a long day of listening to speakers, flopped down into bed to sleep. Sleep never came though, as we stayed up all night gabbing like high school girls at a slumber party, and like high school girls at a slumber party we hit upon the topic of boys; well, in our case, men. I remember what Lyndia said as vividly as I remember the birth of my first child. "I will never marry again," she adamantly proclaimed. Actually, words in print do not do the tone of her voice justice, nor do they adequately describe the vehemence with which she made her proclamation. "I will NEV-ERRR EV-ERRR get married again. I mean it," she stated with such seriousness that I would have believed her, had it not been for the undeniable tug of the Holy Spirit telling me she would eat her words. I am happy to say that I personally witnessed Miss "I mean it" walk down the aisle and marry Mr. "I Proved You Wrong," Don McMillan, just a few months later. Yes, it happened that fast!

Lyndia had been in my Bible Study class and prayer group where we had grown to be dear friends. I watched as my sweet sister in Christ endured the loss of a spouse to illness and due to a charlatan, faced monumental financial burdens as well. Add that to her growing heap of struggles and physical problems and you have a small glimpse of all that had been on Job's, I mean, Lyndia's plate. It was during this period of Lyndia's life that I saw a faith budding that is today ten thousand blooming rose gardens strong. I believe, too, that it is the faith born out of this time period in Lyndia's life, which enabled her to be such a strong fragrance for Christ in difficult times to come.

This book is about those times, but it is so much more. It is not only a journey of hardship, but it is a book which portrays the love of two people for their God and each other.

Lyndia always thought that she and Don McMillan were an unlikely pair. Lyndia had devoted her life to raising her children, working as a secretary, and was/is a wonderful seamstress. Her formal education ended after two semesters of college, but I will say, she continues to be a life-long learner, the pursuit of God her passion. On the other hand, Don had been a world traveled career man with a master's degree. Organized, punctual, and always a perfect gentleman, Don swooped in and, well, the rest is history.

Don began journaling just three days before he and Lyndia married. Although he had been writing letters, instructions, and other documents for many years, Don struggled to put his innermost thoughts down on paper. Although she was aware that Don had a journal, Lyndia didn't actually read it until just a few weeks before his death. She had all but forgotten about its existence. Once Don went home to be with the Lord, Lyndia had the thought of taking the journal to Don Jones, who would be giving Don's eulogy. It was a new experience for Don Jones, never before having been given such access to someone's personal thoughts. It touched everyone sitting in the church pews that day as Don McMillan's very own words became his eulogy.

After the funeral and now back at her house, Lyndia and her granddaughter, Sarah, reviewed the day, with their thoughts resting on Don's journal. It was so rich. So much was there. It felt wrong to tuck the journal away in a box. If the journal were ever published, Sarah contended, she would very much like to read it…and I'm thinking, you will, too.

Aware of her frailties, Lyndia was terrified just thinking about putting her own thoughts down on paper, but in order for the journal to make sense to its reader, she had to do it. Wanting to bring glory and honor to the Lord, Lyndia began the task of reading through and comparing journal entries. Sometimes the process was a painful endeavor, bringing tears to her eyes, and sometimes it was one of joy and laughter. No matter what, Lyndia trudged on, because she believed the Lord had a purpose for the book, for every person that would one day read it. Believing her faith was being put to the test yet again, Lyndia plunged into the work as the clock on the wall ticked away the hours. Somewhere in the process, it occurred to Lyndia that God was using her in spite of her weaknesses so that His strength would be made evident.

In her book, *Unexpected Blessings*, you will journey backwards with Don and Lyndia, visiting moments and circumstances in each of their lives before the Lord brought them together. You will also get to see the making of their marriage, and the faith in Christ which gave it such strength. If you have been broken by past hurts, if today you face painful circumstances or giant hurdles, if you have ever suffered the jarring pain of loss, then this book is sure to minister hope and healing to your heart. If you have ever wondered at the faithfulness of God, or have in times of great sorrow asked yourself, "Does it get any better than this?" then *Unexpected Blessings* will trumpet, "God is faithful," and "Yes, with Jesus, everything gets better."

Catherine Jones

My Journey Of Faith

As I was growing up, going to church on Sunday was always a part of our household routine. Often we attended on Saturday nights as well. Mom and Dad met each other at church, fell in love, and were married. As time elapsed, dad remained at home while Mom took all three of us kids to church. I am grateful for her commitment to the Lord and to us. She faithfully attended service after service despite the empty space in the pew meant for my dad. All that changed when my sister Judi, who was only a year old, was stricken with pneumonia and was hospitalized. At the time, the doctor said her prognosis was rather grim. Judi's illness broke my dad's heart. On top of that, my mom was sick at the same time. You can just imagine how Dad felt with a daughter near death in the hospital and a sick wife at home in bed. One day after checking on Judi, Dad drove home to check on Mom. My mom, who had been praying for my dad's salvation for a very long time, told him that she did not feel Judi would recover unless he gave his life to the Lord. Her words, coupled with the power of the Holy Spirit made an impression. Sensing the Lord was calling him, my dad walked out to his truck, and there in the cab gave his life to Christ. Upon returning to Judi's hospital room, to my dad's amazement, he discovered the Lord had miraculously healed my sister, and she was fine. Dad served God faithfully, and years later, when I was a teenager, he was one of my Sunday school teachers. A godly heritage is a precious gift, and I will always be thankful for the faith of my parents.

In elementary school I came to believe in the Lord as my Savior and was baptized in a river.

As a regular church attendee I can honestly say I don't ever remember hearing about how to have a growing relationship with the Lord. Church was more about behavior and rules, a code of ethics to be followed.

Almost a year after getting married, my husband and I moved to St. Louis and began attending a small Baptist church. Since I had grown up in a different denomination, the pastor of the church spent some time helping me to understand the scriptures a little better. He also encouraged me to attend classes where he taught Biblical doctrine. My baby girl, Shellie was just a few weeks old when I was baptized again. Probably being about the same age as she was spiritually, and not being ready to receive anything stronger, I was one of those believers who have to be fed with milk instead of solid food.

In less than a year we moved back to Muskogee, visited several churches, and decided to join First Baptist Church. My life became very hectic and stressful over the years as I struggled with raising children, working from home and at my job. I wrestled with my own self worth, with my relationship with my husband, and I had no close friendships. I remember a sermon that our pastor preached about a woman who had always worn a mask but one day when she decided to take it off there was no one there. I knew I was that woman. Life seemed like a treadmill. I was always running but going nowhere. Feeling hopeless, alone, insignificant, and defeated, I had allowed the enemy to deceive me. Being easily deceived was a result of my turning inward looking at my problems and hurts instead of focusing on God and His Word. Trusting in my unstable feelings obscured my vision until I could no longer see that Christ wanted me to lay everything at His feet, to completely surrender my old life to Him. God is much greater than my feelings.

From the beginning of my marriage, I knew I had made a mistake, but I was taught that once you were married, you stayed married no matter what. But after 21 years of marriage, I got a divorce. Justifying my decision with all kinds of reasons, I went ahead with my plan, instead of waiting on the Lord and trusting him with the solutions to my problems. Thankfully the Lord was merciful to forgive and to blot out all my sins. I am reminded of Romans 4:7 which says: "Oh, what joy for those whose disobedience is forgiven, whose sins are put out of sight." Not only did the Lord forgive my sins, but instead of answering my rebellion with wrath, He showed me mercy. "The Lord our God is merciful and forgiving, even though we have rebelled against him" (Daniel 9:9).

After my divorce, I joined the singles class at our church, and several months later John Taylor, who had recently moved to Muskogee from Tulsa came to the class for the first time. We kept running into each other that Sunday. Calling the next week, he asked me out and we were married four months later.

It was many years later that I finally began to understand that living a Christian life was so much more than going to church and spending a few minutes a day reading a scripture and a devotional. "I was so foolish and ignorant – I must have seemed like a senseless animal to You. Yet I still belong to You, You hold my right hand. You guide me with Your counsel, leading me to a glorious destiny" (Psalm 73:22).

At work one day, my boss, who also attended our church, told me that his wife Delores had to be at work at 8 a.m. but got up at 5:30 every morning to spend an hour with the Lord. Deciding I needed to spend more time with the Lord, I too began to get up earlier each day to have a quiet time. I realized God was creating in me a hunger for His Word. During one of those times with the Lord, I told Him that I was so sorry for being such a slow learner. Having lived over 50 years and now looking back, I could see I had ignorantly wasted much of my life. Showing me that He was trustworthy, God took me just as I was, with all my failures, stubbornness, and ignorance, transforming me into His likeness. Thankfully God was and is patient, and I finally began to grasp what it meant to live for Christ. In Romans 2:4 the apostle Paul spoke of the wonderful patience of God towards us. "Don't you see how wonderfully kind, tolerant, and patient God is with you? Does this mean nothing to you? Can't you see that His kindness is intended to turn you from your sin?" (Romans 2:4).

Consider the impoverished person who has little contact with his family and friends, refusing to respond to their calls, casually disregarding the cry of their hearts when they speak. The very idea seems horribly sad, uncomfortably wrong, but that is exactly what I had once done to my own heavenly Father. There was a time I had shut out the very One who had created me and given me everything – even eternal life with Him. How could I have thought my few minutes of reading a little scripture and a devotional was all God intended in our relationship? As time unfolded, I came to see that the Lord had in mind so much more. He desired an intimate relationship with me, one that would be a continual growing process lasting until my final breath on earth. He wanted me to know His heart. Through prayer I would learn to pour out my heart to the Father, and I would go to Him on behalf of others. I found that intimacy with God not only involved time with Him, but required confession and repentance on my part; humbling myself before Him, spending significant time in His Word…and listening. A wonderful result of intimacy with God is a changed life but it is something we must permit. Romans 12:2b tells us, "Let God transform you into a new person by changing the way you think. Then you will learn to know God's will for you, which is good and pleasing and perfect." The key word is "let." We have to cooperate with God, allowing His power to conform us into the image of His Son, and allow His thoughts to become ours.

Reading through the Psalms was how I began. One day while shopping for a box of greeting cards, my eyes rested on the rack of journals right in front of me. "Lyndia, you need one of those," I felt the Lord say. Taking the journal, I began to fill it with scriptures that had really spoken to me during my quiet times. Little did I know that they would become the source for my prayers at a pivotal time in my life, when my mom was hospitalized requiring several transfusions because her blood count was significantly low. A day later she suffered a stroke and lay unresponsive in her hospital bed. With many prayer warriors praying the Word over her, I saw God restore mom to life the next day, with only the loss of her peripheral vision in both eyes. Giving God all the credit for her turnaround, we attributed it to the power in praying God's Word.

The scriptures from my quiet time once again became my treasure when my husband was diagnosed with a very rare neurological disease, a brain disease that affected his entire neurological system. The diagnosis was difficult for both of us to process, not knowing what to expect or how to deal with the physical and mental changes taking place in his body. The cruel nature of my husband's incurable disease resulted in the gradual loss of all his motor skills. Akin to having Parkinson's, Alzheimer's, and other neurological diseases all at once, this disease had yet to be named, so the doctors called it Parkinsonism.

Being told he had an incurable disease came with another devastating pronouncement. My husband would no longer be able to drive. Initially he disregarded the neurologist's pleas to not get behind the wheel of a car; that is, until he received a letter in the mail revoking his license. It was not long after the diagnosis that the symptoms of the disease took over and the nightmare began. Hallucinations and schizophrenia captured my husband's mind, carrying the man I knew away from me. Fearing what he might do in his altered state of mind, I found myself caring for my husband around the clock. There was an element of fear involved in his care, fear for his safety and fear for my own. One day my husband was certain there was a body in his bed, alarming me when he said he wanted to shoot it. There was quite a large gun and ammunition collection in the house because at one time my husband had been a highway patrolman. Along with the body in the bed were other hallucinations, or "critters" as he called them, in the room and under the mattress. As he deteriorated physically and emotionally, so did our relationship.

A friend from my Bible study group suggested that scriptures might help to soothe my husband. Printing scriptures large enough for him to read during the night, I put them on the wall near his bed.

Eventually, the day came when the doctor said it was time to place my husband in an assisted living facility. Knowing that the doctor knew better than anyone, yet having a feeling of relief and guilt all at the same time, I agreed to his recommendation.

Being impatient, and not being in God's Word enough to find that place of complete dependence on Christ, I didn't do very well in dealing with my husband or the disease at first. Helplessness and desperation overcame me most of the time, until I finally began seeking the Lord, spending significant time in His Word, and in prayer. As I think of all that could have happened had I not turned to the Lord, I am so grateful that God turned my thoughts toward Him, grateful that He kept me in the palm of His hand. A glance backward reminded me that sometimes God has had to crush me like a lump of clay in order to remake me into His image. The circumstances of my life were mere tools to build His character in me and transform my thinking. Shattered, feeling I had nothing left except the Lord, I found He was all I needed. Jesus said, "If you try to hang on to your life, you will lose it. But if you give up your life for My sake, you will save it" (Luke 9:24).

Long term care of any patient is mentally, emotionally, and physically exhausting, and as the days wore on I began to struggle physically under the stress. New to me were excruciating migraine headaches, a gallbladder attack resulting in surgery, and then a bout of pneumonia. Sometimes I wondered if I would survive. I cried. I prayed, and I asked God when it would all end. Today I can take refuge in Romans 2:12 which states: "Rejoice in our confident hope. Be patient in trouble, and keep on praying." Today, I can look at that trying time and view it as a treasure because the end result is that I gained Christ. I have come to know that God wants the full attention of His children and He certainly got mine. Now He is my priority. For me the words of the psalmist ring true: "My suffering was good for me for it taught me to pay attention to Your decrees. Your instructions are more valuable to me than millions in gold and silver" (Psalm119:71). If suffering and affliction resulted in my knowing God through His Word, it was a small price to pay for such great gain.

There's more. In February of 2000, soon after my husband's diagnosis, my dad was diagnosed with liver cancer, and before we could absorb the gravity of the news, he died, just three weeks later. At the time, I had been working for him at Bruce's Poultry, a business he had started approximately 35 years before. Being the only one in our family who knew at least a little about the business, I tried to keep it afloat after Dad was gone, but it became evident we really needed to sell it. One day a man called expressing interest in purchasing the business, and after looking it over he told me he was ready to buy it. Calling on the opinions of several people, including my mother, officers at the bank, our attorney and our accountant, we concluded the offer was legitimate and sounded good. It wasn't until much later that we learned the man had been stealing small businesses all over the United States, and ours was one of them. His underhandedness resulted in my elderly mother having to live on her meager social security each month and not having enough income to pay for all her medications. As her financial situation worsened, she was forced to sell her home and move to a much older and smaller house.

One thing I love about the Psalms is that they speak of the human condition. They express the emotions of very real people crying out in desperation to a very real God. In his distress, David cried out, "Lord, don't hold back Your tender mercies from me. My only hope is in Your unfailing love and faithfulness. For troubles surround me – too many to count! They pile up so high I can't see my way out. They are more numerous than the hairs on my head. I have lost all my courage. Please, Lord, rescue me! Come quickly, Lord, and help me" (Psalm 40:11-12). David's cries to the Lord became my cries, "Lord, don't hold back Your tender mercies from me…" With so many troubles all at once, you can imagine how distraught I was becoming.

Sometimes our trials seem to last indefinitely, and if we are not careful we will let them define our lives. In 2 Corinthians 4:17, the apostle Paul reminds us to compare the trying times against eternity, and to focus on the end result. "For our present troubles are small and won't last very long. Yet they produce for us a glory that vastly outweighs them and will last forever" (2 Corinthians 4:17). I have come to understand that if God permits a problem in my life, it has a purpose, to produce a glory that is heavier than the weight of my trials and that lasts for eternity.

During the first five or six years of my husband's illness, when I could still leave him alone, I began attending a small group Bible study. Being rather shy and not really knowing how to form intimate relationships resulted in my having no close friendships. I don't know exactly why, but the feeling of inferiority had plagued me my whole life. Sweetly, the Lord used the Bible study to bless me with friends, friends who not only encouraged me but lifted me up in prayer.

My husband died March 3, 2005, and my mom passed away the same year on December 7. Although their deaths were a huge loss, I thrust myself upon the Lord and He sustained me, enabling me to live beyond my grief. In Philippians 4:12-13, Paul said, "I have learned the secret of living in every situation...for I can do everything through Christ, who gives me strength." I think it is worth noting that the secret to living in every situation has to be "learned." Every believer has to learn for himself that he can do everything *through* Christ, who is the giver of strength. There is no other way.

In her book, *Streams in the Desert*, L.B. Cowman quoted Henry Ward Beecher as saying, "Never fear the fierce storms that even now may be blowing through your life. Storms bring blessings and rich fruit will be harvested later." If we would but trust God to see us through every difficulty and keep in mind the end result, a harvest of rich fruit, every trial would then become something of great value to us.

God's Word sustained me. The Lord reminded me that He was my royal husband, and I would continually have His presence, His comfort, His help, and His love. John, the beloved disciple wrote, "See how very much our Father loves us, for He calls us His children, and that is what we are" (I John 3:1). Oh, if only we would see! If only we would grasp how deeply God loves us as a father tenderly loves his children. His love is unlike any other love we have ever known. "For his unfailing love toward those who fear Him is as great as the height of the heavens above the earth. He has removed our sins as far from us as the east is from the west. The Lord is like a father to His children, tender and compassionate to those who fear Him. For He knows how weak we are; He remembers we are only dust" (Psalm 103:11-14). More often than not, we fear the problems before us rather than have a reverential fear of the Lord. If we would alter that, fear God instead, then we would have an awareness of His love and forgiveness, and no struggle would overtake us.

Had it not been for the Word that I read each morning during my quiet time, I couldn't have made it through those really tough times. Like David, "I saw only trouble and sorrow. Then I called on the name of the Lord. Please, Lord, save me! How kind the Lord is! How good He is! So merciful, this God of ours!" (Psalm 116:3b-5). The Lord gave me strength for each day. As I began to cry out to the Lord, thinking I couldn't take any more, I prayed for Him to just take me on home. Now I realize that He knew exactly where I was and where He was taking me. I was learning to know Him and trust Him more because He was all I had. My circumstances were a mess, but God carried me through, refined, and transformed me.

At times I could hear God's gentle whispers, His still small voice. When I couldn't sleep, He gave me songs in the night: "In His Time" (He makes everything beautiful in His time) and "Precious Lord, Take My Hand." He assured me he would never leave me or forsake me, and that I could make it with His help. Having no strength of my own, He gave me His strength in exchange for my weaknesses. God's Word became my treasure. I believe had it not been for all of my problems, I would not have learned to love God's Word or to trust Him like I do. I know that I can do nothing apart from Him. Christ in me.

In her book, *Streams in the Desert*, Mrs. L. B. Cowman wrote, "If God has called us to His highest and best, each of us will have a time of crisis, when all our resources will fail, and when we face either ruin, or something better than we have ever dreamed. But before we can receive the blessing, we must rely on God's infinite help. We must be willing to let go, surrendering completely to Him, and cease from our own wisdom, strength, and righteousness. We must be 'crucified with Christ' (Galatians 2:20) and yet alive in Him. God knows how to lead us to the point of crisis, and He knows how to lead us through it." My Heavenly Father was faithful to lead me all the way.

Nothing in my life today is more satisfying than my relationship with the Lord. He never stops loving me and knows all my thoughts and feelings. I can only praise Him, for He forgives me, heals my hurts, and gives me hope. To top it off, He is preparing a place for me where I will be with Him for eternity. More than anything, I desire that my life be an expression of gratefulness for all that my Lord has done in me and for me. "What counts is whether we have been transformed into a new creation" (Galatians 6:15). This life I now live is not of my making but is because of the cross of Jesus Christ. To borrow the apostle, Paul's words, "May

I never boast about anything except the cross of our Lord Jesus Christ" (Galatians 6:14a).

After John's death in 2005, being very adamant, I vowed I would <u>never</u> have another relationship with a man or marry again. My friend Catherine reminded me quite often of our conversation when I said, "I'll never." Never is a word I'm very reluctant to use these days, since every time I have said never, the Lord has brought about circumstances to change my never to, "whatever you want Lord."

When the Lord brought Don into my life I thankfully relinquished my Never to Whatever you want Lord. We were married July 22, 2006.

Don and I had been married just a few months when I got a call from an FBI agent. The agent wanted me to testify for the FBI in United States District Court against the man who had stolen my dad's business. Fearing I would be so nervous that I wouldn't be able to speak, I simply didn't want to testify. Maybe you know this by now, but God has an uncanny way of stretching us beyond snapping, calling us to face the very giants from which we would rather hide. If God calls us up to face some fear, He wants us to be aware of His power and rely on it at that moment. When Timothy wrote, "God has not given us a spirit of fear and timidity, but of power, love, and self-discipline" (2 Timothy 1:7), he pointed out that fear does not originate with God. God does not intimidate those He loves, but instead endues them with power. It would not be long before I would come to know what it meant to be filled with the power of God instead of fear.

We were in Branson the day the FBI agent called to confirm my trip to Virginia to testify in U.S. District Court, but I didn't check my cell phone until the next day. During my quiet time that morning, I had read from Jeremiah 1 where God told Jeremiah, "...you must go wherever I send you and say whatever I tell you. And don't be afraid of the people, for I will be with you and will protect you. I, the Lord, have spoken! Then the Lord reached out and touched my mouth and said, 'Look, I have put my words in your mouth'" (Jeremiah 1:7-9).

My immediate thought was, "Lord, I'm going to have to testify, aren't I?" I called the FBI agent and agreed to testify. I was still nervous, but I knew the Lord wanted me to just trust Him.

I was very thankful that Don accompanied me to Norfolk. Before court, I spent some time talking to the attorney and FBI agent. The attorney reviewed the questions he would later ask me in court before a judge. Encouraged by the Word God had given me in preparation for this day, I found that I wasn't a bit nervous.

When it was time to go forward to testify, my knees did not shake, my voice did not quiver, and I spoke without fear or intimidation. Because the Lord truly did put the words in my mouth, gone was the fear of man. At the end of the hearing, I was asked if I would like to say something directly to the man, who because of his thievery had caused such pain and difficulty to my family. Once again I stood before the court and addressed the man who once was arrogant but now seemed broken, telling him how my mom had fervently prayed for him right up until she died. I told him that I too, prayed for him, and that what he had done had been very hard on all of us, particularly my elderly mother. Taking my cue from scripture, I told the man that what he had meant for harm God had turned around and used for my good, and ended my address with the words, "I forgive you." I had released my perpetrator and it felt so good. "If you forgive those who sin against you, your heavenly Father will forgive you. But if you refuse to forgive others, your Father will not forgive your sins" (Matthew 6:14). How could I hold this man's sins against him when my heavenly Father had forgiven me of all my sins?

After testifying in court, Don and I ate lunch with the FBI agent and attorney along with two other men who were also victims. Surprised that I had forgiven the man whose crime had brought us all together, and calling me an inspiration for doing so, the men revealed that they hadn't considered forgiving their perpetrator but now realized the necessity of it. In stepping out and trusting God to fill me with His power that I might testify in U.S. District Court, I wound up being a witness for the Lord. What if I had embraced my fears and let them prevent me from speaking, openly offering forgiveness?

From Lyndia's Journal

*R*eading through my journal entries from a few months before Don and I were married, I was amazed when I realized how God had answered my prayers. I'm sure the entries were a result of the Holy Spirit's enlightenment of scripture or a devotional that I had read that particular day.

May 4, 2006

Father, help me to live in constant fellowship with Christ and give me Your direction and leadership in the fulfillment of Your plan. Help me to seek Your guidance in all decisions. Thank you Lord for sharing Your secrets with me. Thank you for redemption and transformation. I am determined to be identified with Christ. Make me a significant contact in the lives of others.

(Many important decisions that I would have to make were just ahead, and I would be made a significant contact in Don's life.)

May 9, 2006

"He will order His angels to protect you wherever you go" (Psalm 91:11).

Father, help me to keep Christ in my vision and to expect greater things. Increase my faith and help me to always look to You.

You are an awesome God. Thank you that Your blessings are eternal.

(Greater things were definitely on the way.)

May 19, 2006

Thank you that nothing can separate me from the love of God in Christ Jesus, that I am more than a conqueror even in the midst of terrible circumstances.

"Can anything ever separate us from Christ's love?" "No, despite all these things, overwhelming victory is ours through Christ, who loved us" (Romans 8:35, 37).

(Reminding me of His great love, God was in the process of healing the hurts of my heart and transforming my thoughts. At the time, I had no idea He was healing a past and also preparing me for a future filled with joy as well as sorrow. This time the sorrows I would encounter did not cripple me but only served to draw me closer to the Lord. I did not become a servant to grief, but rather grief became my servant, leading me to my Master's feet.)

May 25, 2006

Thank you, Lord that You are my Master. All the good things I have come from You. You alone are my inheritance, my cup of blessing. You guard all that is mine. You are always with me, guiding me and instructing me. You show me the way of life granting me the joy of Your presence and the pleasures of living with You forever. (Psalm 16:11)

Help me to choose the best that You have for me: Your will. I allow You to make Your choice for me. Help me to live having my eyes focused on You.

May 29, 2006

Help me to praise You publicly, and when I complain, may it be only to You. Thank you for holding me in Your hand. Help me to wait patiently on You. Help me to be disciplined in every area of my life so I will be Your faithful follower.

(This was probably when I was complaining to Don, ranting and raving about a situation, not realizing that the Lord was already at work, and would use the situation to bring about His plan.)

May 30, 2006

Thank you for always hearing me Lord. Thank you for forgiving my past, healing the present, and giving me hope for the future. I am determined to give myself to You in total surrender, but I need Your help Father. I trust You completely. I am willing to invest my faith in Your character.

(My trust was not as complete as I thought.)

June 4, 2006

Thank you for the Holy Spirit within, who leads me into all truth revealing Jesus to me. Thank you for guiding me even in my everyday choices and in common sense. Help me to be aware of being guided by You. Help me to always listen to You. I know You will never leave me or forsake me.

"Who are those who fear the Lord? He will show them the path they should choose" (Psalm 25:12).

"I will never fail you. I will never forsake you" (Hebrews 13:5).

June 5, 2006

Help me to measure everything in life by Your truth. I praise You, Father. You are Awesome, You are Holy, You are Truth, You are Love and everything that is good, my All in All. Thank you for being my friend, and giving me Christian friends.

(This entry reminds me of how the Lord brought my much loved friend Becky into my life when we just happened to sit at the same table one Wednesday night. I believe the Lord knew that each of us needed a close friend. We agreed to encourage and hold one another accountable. Becky epitomizes a loyal friend, a true sister in Christ. She is a faithful, cherished friend who continues to uphold me with her help, prayers, encouragement, and love.)

Thank you for bearing all my sins and grief. Help me to remember that You are a huge God, bigger than any fear, circumstance, trial, or illness, or grief.

June 6, 2006

Father, help me to have an eternal perspective. Show me where to walk, teach me to do Your will, and lead me by Your gracious Spirit. You, Lord, are my rock. You give me strength for battle and stand before me. You are great and worthy of praise. Your greatness is beyond comprehension! I pray that my children and grandchildren will realize Your greatness, that they will meditate on Your majestic, glorious splendor, share the story of Your wonderful goodness, and sing with the joy of Your righteousness.

"Teach me to do Your will, for You are my God. May Your gracious Spirit lead me forward on a firm footing" (Psalm 143:10).

Thank you that you shower compassion on all Your creation. You are faithful in all You say and gracious in all You do. You lift those bent beneath their loads. Thank you for being close to all you call on You.

Give me spiritual discernment. Help me to be something I have never been. Fulfill Your purpose in me.

(What was I thinking, praying for the Lord to make me into something I had never been? How was I to know that my beloved husband would go through the fire of affliction, and I would go through it with Him? The Lord certainly did and He graciously prepared me through His Word. How could I have known that He would call upon me to write a book? It's difficult for me to comprehend. Knowing I was not capable to do anything apart from Him, I lay my life in the Lord's hands and followed His lead.)

June 16, 2006

Help me to be a loyal friend, give me a cheerful heart, help me to keep my eyes glued on wisdom, and give me understanding. Help me to know when to speak and when to be silent. Let the words of my mouth be as life-giving refreshing water. Help me to be a good listener. Let my tongue nourish life. Help me not to judge or criticize others.

"Since the first day you began to pray for understanding and to humble yourself before your God, your request has been heard in heaven" (Daniel 10:12).

"A friend is always loyal" (Proverbs 17:17).

June 21, 2006

Father, let me be clothed with strength and dignity. Help me to be kind. I want to be a woman who fears You and is in a right relationship with You, always growing.

"She is clothed with strength and dignity and she laughs with no fear of the future" (Proverbs 31:25).

June 22, 2006

Father, help me to trust You with all my heart and in all my ways, and to seek Your will in all I do.

"Trust in the Lord with all your heart; do not depend on your own understanding. Seek His will in all you do, and He will show you which path to take" (Proverbs 3:5-6).

Help me to wait on You Lord, so I can know Your direction for my life.

June 23-24, 2006

The Beth Moore conference was great; all about trust from Psalm 115.

"All you who fear the Lord, trust the Lord! He is your help and your shield" (Psalm 115:11).

(The conference was life changing, a struggle and yet a rich blessing. Isn't that how our Lord usually works? As I am so slow to learn, He most usually has to work that way in me.)

June 25, 2006

My prayer just after the Beth Moore conference: I confess distrust. I want to trust You with every area of my life, every relationship, circumstance, service, security, and all of life. I want to keep the shield of faith (trust) always over my heart so the enemy will grieve. Bless others through me.

June 26, 2006

I want to be yielded to Your authority and trust You for guidance. Give me the desire to do Your will and obey Your commands. Uphold my cause. I want to be faithful to You, Lord, my God. Transform my heart and my mind. I seek Your will in every decision. Help me to always seek Your will and guide me for Your way is best, Father. Help me to love and bless others; to be pure and virtuous.

I talked with Don McMillan today. His friendship is such a blessing, and I really enjoy his company.

(This entry was Monday, following the Beth Moore conference, the day our lives would drastically change. I was very excited, apprehensive, but not quite sure of Don's reaction.)

June 27, 2006

I want to use the weapons You have given me that are mighty in bringing down strongholds, and I want to bring every thought captive to the obedience of Christ.

"We use God's mighty weapons…to knock down the strongholds of human reasoning…" (Corinthians 10:4).

"We capture their rebellious thoughts and teach them to obey Christ" (I Corinthians 10:5b).

TRUST-means to trust, rely on, put confidence in, secure, to lead to believe.

June 28, 2006

"Let the Word of Christ dwell in you richly in all wisdom" (Colossians 3:16).

Thank you, Jesus Christ for replacing my sin with the glorious robe of Your righteousness.

"…I am still not all I should be, but I am focusing all my energies on this one thing: Forgetting the past and looking forward to what lies ahead. I strain to reach the end of the race and receive the prize for which God, through Jesus Christ, is calling us up to heaven" (Philippians 3:13-14).

Father, help me to be consistent in obeying the truth I have already learned.

(Still dealing with all the difficulties from the past but, thankfully, I know the Lord will help me to forget the past and look forward to what is ahead.)

June 29, 2006

I want to walk in the fear of the Lord and in the comfort of the Holy Spirit. Perfect in me Your will and plan for my life.

Don McMillan took me to breakfast and for a drive today. We talked and talked. He is so nice.

(This was our first "date." I feel giddy just thinking about it, and I am smiling.)

July 1, 2006

Help me to believe You, Father, not just believe in You. You are in control of all situations.

Don took me to see a movie and to dinner. Thank you, Lord, for this unexpected blessing. We prayed together before we left. Help me to fully trust You, Lord, with this relationship.

Don told me that he loves me.

(I was still learning how much the Lord loved me, and I was excited to know that Don loved me, too.)

July 2, 2006

Father, go before us to lead the way. Help us not to run ahead of You, to let You do it all. Help us to stay true to You.

I want to be strong in faith and full of the Holy Spirit. I know You are telling me to trust You and allow You to take care of all the details. Heal my wounds Lord, as only You can. Thank you for bringing this precious man into my life.

Thank you for giving me a passionate love for my Lord Jesus through the Holy Spirit. Thank you for taking my entire being and setting me ablaze with glowing devotion to Jesus Christ. Help me to be consistent in my relationship to You, Lord. Fill me with Your Spirit. I don't want just a cup. I am consumed with You; I worship You. Thank you for healing my wounds, and helping me to trust You. I'm sorry, Lord, that I have been so slow to learn. Help me to get it!

July 3, 2006

Father, help me to always depend on You and to keep growing closer to You. Apart from You I can do nothing. I need Your guidance in everything. I want to be obedient and follow You with all my heart, and do whatever You want me to do. I want to remain faithful to You throughout my life. Reveal the sin in me. I want be thoroughly clean and pure before You. Forgive my distrust.

Don took me to Braum's again. He knows that frozen yogurt is my weakness.

Thank you Father for this relationship that You had to sneak in on me. You must be very amused. Help me to stay in right relationship with You and wait on You. Guard my heart and mind in Christ Jesus. I pray that both Don and I would keep You at the center of our lives and give top priority to our relationship with You.

Don took me to Tulsa for the July 4th celebration at Liberty Baptist Church. He is such a precious, sweet man. Thank you, Lord, for this wonderful gift and how You engineered it all. You are incredible, Lord.

(With our relationship being so new and because of my shyness, I have to admit that being with some of Don's family at the July 4th celebration was a little uncomfortable, but it was because of me, not them.)

July 5, 2006

Father, I pray that my life would demonstrate Your grace and righteousness. I want to live by faith. Forgive my distrust and every doubt along the way. Thank you, Lord, for Your gentle whispers.

Help me to commit my way to You, Lord, to trust in You, for You have said that You will bring it to pass.

"Commit everything you do to the Lord. Trust Him, and He will help you" (Psalm 37:5).

Father, You are completely amazing! Thank you for using me to share with others what You have done.

Don and I talked for a while in the Chapel. Don said to me, "This is where I want us to get married."

Father, You are already binding up my wounds, healing my hurts, and replacing my fear with Your perfect love. Thank you for restoration and refreshing, and for giving me back my life again. Thank you that I am in Your hands no matter what others may say. Thank you for helping me to learn humble submission to Your will and help me to wait patiently on You.

July 6, 2006

Don took me to Van Buren to look around the shops and just be together.

(Each time Don and I were together, we were more relaxed with one another, always finding something to talk about.)

July 7, 2006

Thank you, Father for increasing my faith, and helping me to have endurance. Grow my faith (trust) so I will be strong in character and ready for anything.

Thank you that I am Your choice possession. Help me to be quick to listen, slow to speak, and slow to get angry. I humbly accept the message You have planted in my heart. Help me to remember that it is a message to obey. I want to keep looking steadily into Your perfect law. I refuse to let the world corrupt me.

"You must be quick to listen, slow to speak, and slow to get angry"
(James 1:19),

Thank you for guiding me, charting the path ahead of me, and for preceding me and following me. Thank you for supporting me with Your strength, for thinking about me, and being with me.

Don asked me to marry him today, July 7, 2006. Of course I said, "YES!" We planned our wedding for July 22, 2006. This whole thing was God's idea, so with no doubt, why not get on with this plan of God. Father, I want to try to express my thanks to You for the very special gift of the most wonderful, kind, sweet, incredible, loving, and precious man that You have given me. He is unique, and it's as if You made him especially for me. Help me to grow steadily in my relationship with You, but also with him. Thank you that we can pray together, talk about Your Word, and are connected by You. Thank you for healing my wounds so that I can enter into this marriage with freedom. You amaze and thrill me, Father. I want to know You more and more and more.

I am overwhelmed with gratitude to You, Lord. Thank you for giving us back our lives again in the land of the living, and also for the hope of the future You have planned for us.

(My friend Catherine reminded me that it is amazing how God takes our "I'll never" and turns it into "Of course, I will.")

July 8, 2006

Make me rich in faith. Help me to be as merciful to others as You are merciful to me. Let my actions prove my faith. I want to trust You so much, Lord, that I am willing to go and do whatever You tell me. I want my faith to be complete by my actions.

His [Abraham's] faith and his actions worked together. His actions made his faith complete" (James 4:22).

Thank you for feeling what I feel. Thank you that I can bring anything and everything to You in prayer, for You truly understand and Your compassions never fail.

July 11.2006

Father, keep me spiritually healthy. Your plan will end in good, for You are tender and merciful. I want to keep praying and being thankful, continually singing praises to You, Lord.

Thank you for revealing Your truth to me through the living Word, and the assurance that I can absolutely depend on Christ.

"Now to him who is able to do far more abundantly beyond all that we ask or think, according to the power that works within us" (Ephesians 3:20).

Help me to not settle for less than what You intend.

July 12, 2006

I am determined to seek You with all my heart, and build my relationship with You first and foremost. Help Don and me to remember that our relationship with each other is dependent on our relationship with You.

July 13, 2006

Help me to grow in You, and be conformed to the likeness of Christ. Thank you for divine appointments.

Thank you for bringing Don into my life.

July 14, 2006

Father, Your Word says that You reveal Your every thought. How awesome You are, Lord. Thank you that I can share eternal life through Christ. Thank you for choosing and calling me even before I was born. What underserved mercy! Thank you for revealing Your Son to me.

"Who can know what the Lord is thinking? Who can give Him counsel? But we can understand these things, for we have the mind of Christ" (I Corinthians 2:16).

We got our marriage license today.

(This was really happening! It wasn't a dream! Don consulted with me about everything, but he was the real wedding planner. He wanted our wedding to be really special. Not wasting any time, we went to the Court House to get our marriage license at least a week or more before our wedding.)

July 15, 2006

O Father, help me to always be able to hear Your words. I love Your precious Word and it is nourishment for my soul; sweeter than honey. But for Your Word, I would have given up and died. It has sustained me.

Thank you that Christ lives in me. I am trusting in Your Son, who loved me and gave himself for me. Thank you, Jesus, that You died for me.

We made a quick trip to Miami so Don could meet my daughter Shellie and her family. Later that evening, we went to Golden Corral in Muskogee where I was welcomed into the McMillan family.

(Don's family was so gracious to me. They were probably still a little shocked, but they didn't show it. I was still in shock!)

July 16, 2006

Thank you Father, for Your promises. Help me to keep my mind filled with the concept that You are in control of everything, and help me to maintain an attitude of perfect trust in You. Thank you that You have taken hurtful experiences from the past, using them to make me into a better person today, one trying to totally depend on You.

(I never dreamed that God would bless me so much! I don't think I even knew such blessings existed. The song "I Can Only Imagine" comes to mind.)

July 19, 2006

Help me to stay humble before You, Lord. Forgive my distrust and doubt, for I know that it does not come from You. I confess it to You. I want to keep Your shield of faith over my heart. Take control of me today, fill me. I am determined to be found faithful, to be a woman who turns to the Lord with all her heart, soul, strength, and obedience. I want to live to please the Spirit. Thank you that I am a new person in Christ.

"I am certain that God, who began the good work within you, will continue his work until it is finally finished on the day when Christ Jesus returns" (Philippians 1:6).

We picked up our matching rings today. They are gorgeous.

July 20, 2006

Father, I pray that my identity would come only from You. Help me to keep You continually before me. I place my trust in the reality of Your presence. Thank You for directing me, that You bring restraint to my spirit when I make a decision not according to Your will. Help me to be quiet and wait for Your direction.

"But those who trust in the Lord will find new strength. They will soar high on wings like eagles. They will run and not grow weary. They will walk and not faint" (Isaiah 40:31).

Don and I talked to Lance about our wedding.

(Pastor Lance was happy for us. We shared with him that we wanted our wedding to bring glory to our Lord.)

July 21, 2006

Father, I want to thank you once again for the special blessing of bringing Don into my life. Thank you that because of our relationship with You I believe we are prepared to begin our lives together. As our relationship with You grows, let us also grow in our relationship with one another. Thank you that we can pray with one another with freedom and openness; that there is such a completeness in our hearts. Thank you for a new beginning, ordained and orchestrated by You. Thank you for preparing our hearts, for leading us in every step, and for bringing about Your will for us. Don calls it a wellspring of love. How fitting! Thank you for the life giving wellspring of Your love for us and for the love we have for You and for one another.

"The Lord directs our steps, so why try to understand everything along the way?" (Proverbs 20:24).

I met more of Don's family, his brother Myron, and Myron's son Tom from Kansas City.

July 22, 2006

"For the Word of the Lord holds true, and everything He does is worthy of our trust" (Psalm 33:4).

I pray that my life will always honor Christ. I want to boast about what Christ Jesus has done. Thank you for wanting to lift us above ourselves, to want us to see everything in light of Your plans.

Father, thank you that this is our wedding day, and for how You have planned every step. You have truly orchestrated our lives and will continue to do so. Such wonderful blessings You have given us, Lord.

I pray that we would always put You first in our lives. I didn't know it was possible to love a man as deeply and as completely as I love Don.

I know it is only because of what You have done in me. I praise You, Lord. I pray Your blessings upon our marriage. I pray that our marriage would bring honor and glory to Your name and would be a witness to Your power and love for us.

Thank you, Father for our beautiful wedding with all our friends and family. What a blessing! Help my children to understand that our marriage was Your plan, and to see what a wonderful Christian man Don is, and how he loves and cherishes me.

(Don and I wanted our wedding to be a celebration of what the Lord had done in each of us individually, and in bringing us together. Don thought it should be really special, and I believe he accomplished a very special day! We were so thankful for all our family and friends who celebrated with us.)

July 24, 2006

Steady me and make me strong, Lord. Blessed be the Lord, forever. Thank you for refreshing me by Your power.

"You thrill me, Lord, with all You have done for me! I sing for joy because of what You have done" (Psalm 92:4).

Father, I put no confidence in human effort, but instead boast about what Christ has done. There is priceless gain in knowing Christ and becoming one with Him. Thank you that I can really know Christ and experience the mighty power that raised Him from the dead.

Help me to obey the truth I have already learned. Thank you that I am a citizen of heaven. Let others see Christ's gentleness and compassion in me. Remake me within so I am as pure and simple as a child. Thank you for changing my heredity. I am God's child.

"He said to them, 'Let the children come to me. Don't stop them! For the Kingdom of God belongs to such as these. I assure you, anyone who doesn't have their kind of faith will never get into the Kingdom of God'" (Mark 10:14-15).

(Don and I both agreed that our morning quiet time should be a priority, so we began right away.)

July 26, 2006

Father, the gifts that You give are exceptional. Thank you that Don and I have such a complete relationship that we can pray together, encourage one another, talk about Your Word, and have such freedom. Help us to grow closer to You.

Don and I went to Oklahoma City to meet my aunts. They were quite impressed with him.

July 29, 2006

"Our purpose is to please God, not people. He is the one who examines the motives of our hearts" (I Thessalonians 2:4b).

(Our first week as man and wife was incredible. I didn't know that a man as wonderful as Don existed. He is as much a gentleman around the house as he is in public.)

July 31, 2006

"This is the Lord's doing and it is marvelous to see" (Psalm 118:23).

Father I want to become entirely Yours.

August 1, 2006

"Always be joyful. Keep on praying. No matter what happens, always be thankful, for this is God's will for you who belong to Christ Jesus. Hold on to what is good" (I Thessalonians 5:16-19).

"Now may the God of peace make you holy in every way, and may your whole spirit and soul and body be kept blameless until our Lord Jesus Christ comes again. God will make this happen, for He who calls you is faithful" (I Thessalonians 5:23-24).

"Wait on the Lord, and He will work" (Psalm 37:34).

Thank you for the kind of relationship that You have given Don and me. It is so wonderful to be able to share our very hearts and allow Your Holy Spirit to work in us. Thank you for transforming my thoughts and bringing me in line with Your will.

August 2, 2006

"I rejoice in Your Word like one who finds a great treasure" (Psalm 119:162).

August 14, 2006

Father, thank you for looking at my potential instead of my imperfections; thank you that You nurture and transform me into Christ's glorious image.

Thank you for the wonderful blessings You have given me: for Don, for my children, my grandchildren, my family, for providing for me, for bringing many Christian friends into my life, for my church family, for health, and everything else. You have more than met all my needs.

August 18, 2006

We walk by faith, not by sight. Help me to remember that, Father, especially when Don's blood pressure is too high.

"My righteous ones will live by faith" (Hebrews 10:38).

(When Don began having some chest pain, we made an appointment for him to see his cardiologist. There didn't seem to be an immediate problem, but in April of 2007, Don had an angiogram, and we were told that they were unable to put in a stent. He wrote about how disappointed he was in his journal. Having another angiogram the next year, the doctor was able to put a stent in one of Don's God-given arteries. I believe the Lord made it possible. God wasn't ready for him yet.)

August 21, 2006

"My grace is sufficient for you, for my strength is made perfect in weakness. For when I am weak, then I am strong" (2 Corinthians 23:9, 10b).

September 29, 2006

You have comforted Your people and You have compassion on them in their sorrow. You have written my name on Your hand. (Isaiah 49)

October 12, 2006

Let Your Spirit change my way of looking at things.

(The FBI agent called wanting me to testify in court in Virginia.)

October 22, 2006

"I depend on Christ's mighty power that works within me" (Colossians 1:29b).

Don and I have been married three months today. What a blessing!

(Having been married only three months, communication between us was as if we had been married for years. We were able to talk about anything and almost knew what the other was thinking. It was wonderful to be able to talk about the scriptures we had read. I learned about relationship as it was meant to be.)

November 2, 2006

I pray that my body, my soul, my thoughts, and all that I am will be purified and undefiled. Give me one heart and one mind to worship You forever. Let me reflect the glory of Christ. Help me to move ahead not giving in to my weaknesses but doing the right things in spite of my fears or feelings. I want to cooperate with the Holy Spirit. Let me see things from Your perspective and welcome Your promises. I'm looking for a better place, a heavenly home. Thank you for preparing a heavenly city for me.

(From the beginning of our marriage I had committed Don to the Lord. I knew his age and about his heart problem, that there was a possibility that I might not have him a long time, but I knew that what time we did have was because the Lord had given it. We agreed to live every day as if it were our last, making the most of the time we had together. Neither of us knew the day when the Lord would take one of us home.)

November 26, 2006

I pray that I would be known for the beauty from within that comes from You, the beauty of a gentle and quiet spirit.

"You should clothe yourselves instead with the beauty that comes from within, the unfading beauty of a gentle and quiet spirit, which is so precious to God" (I Peter 3:4).

December 5, 2006

Help me to be diligent in confessing my sins to You so I can always be clothed in Christ's righteousness. I pray that I will not be overcome by temptation or Satan's wiles or deceit. Help me to keep my eyes fixed on Jesus, to keep running toward the prize ahead, and to not give up. Help me to not be filled with the worries of this life, but instead, let me be continually filled with the Holy Spirit's power. Thank you for the way of peace.

"If you think you are standing strong, be careful not to fall. The temptations in your life are no different from what others experience. And God is faithful. He will not allow the temptation to be more than you can stand. When you are tempted, He will show you a way out so that you can endure" (I Corinthians 10:12-13).

(We flew to Virginia on December 13, 2006 for the court date on December 14, 2006.)

Skipping approximately three years, the next journal entries begin a few weeks before Don's illness and hospitalization.

December 26, 2009

"You have been given not only the privilege of trusting in Christ but also the privilege of suffering for Him" (Philippians 1:29).

December 28, 2009

(Don added a postscript to a *copy* of the letter he sent to me on July 1, 2006, which was just a few weeks before our wedding. He gave it to me on December 28, 2009. ("PS: You cannot imagine the joy, peace, and thanksgiving I feel today. After 41 months of being your Husband, the excitement and love has only grown. I love you, Darling.")

(He added another postscript Sunday, January 4, 2009, three days before going to the hospital. "PS: My joy is greater, my zest for living has increased, and I want to live as never before.")

"The human spirit can endure a sick body, but who can bear a crushed spirit?" (Proverbs 18:14).

January 7, 2010

(Don was hospitalized January 7, 2011 and was never well enough to return to his earthly home, but instead was taken to his heavenly home May 22, 2010. Somehow I am envious.)

January 9, 2010

"God has said, 'I will never fail you. I will never abandon you'" (Hebrews 13:5).

January 15, 2010

"For no one is abandoned by the Lord forever. Though He brings grief, He also shows compassion because of the greatness of His unfailing love (or mercies). For He does not enjoy hurting (or afflicting) people, or causing them sorrow" (Lamentations 3:31-33).

"But as for me, I know that my Redeemer lives and He will stand upon the earth at last. And after my body has decayed, yet in my body I will see God! I will see Him for myself. Yes, I will see Him with my own eyes. I am overwhelmed at the thought!" (Job 19:25-27).

"You know with all your heart and soul that not one of all the good promises the Lord Your God gave you has failed. Every promise has been fulfilled; not one has failed" (Joshua 23:14).

"Take to heart all the words I have solemnly declared to you this day...They are not just idle words for you – they are your life" (Deuteronomy 32:46-47).

"The Lord always keeps His promises; He is gracious in all He does. The Lord helps the fallen and lifts those bent beneath their loads" (Psalm 145:13b-14).

January 16, 2010

"Then Jesus said, 'Come to Me, all you who are weary and carry heavy burdens and I will give you rest'" (Matthew 11:28).

"Whatever happens…rejoice in the Lord" (Philippians 3:1).

"'I myself will help you', declares the Lord" (Isaiah 41:14).

"So do not fear, for I am with you; do not be dismayed, for I am your God. I will strengthen you and help you" (Isaiah 41:10).

(Notes from Job 39: "Suffering causes us to trust God for who He is, not what He does.")

(Don's first surgery to remove his gallbladder was January 20, 2010.)

January 27, 2010

"When you pass through the waters, I will be with you" (Isaiah 43:2).

(Because of being dehydrated Don was given a large amount of fluid which then caused fluid overload. It was difficult to balance the fluid intake because of the problems with both his heart and his kidneys.)

"The Lord is my strength and my song" (Exodus 15:2). "I will not forget you" (Isaiah 49:15).

(One morning after I had stayed at the hospital all night, Don told me that he had a dream that he wasn't going to make it. He wanted me to remember how much he loved me. This was another time when I was speechless, but this time it was because of my tears. I really wanted him to get better, but deep down, I knew that he might not.)

February 11, 2010

(Friends from church, Don and Sharon Hendrix visited Don at St. Francis Hospital.)

February 12, 2010

"Your heavenly Father knows" (Matthew 6:32).

(Don's granddaughter Julie, knowing her Grandpa would want me to have a Valentine's Day card, bought one, and sent it to the hospital for me. It was so sweet of her.)

February 20, 2010

"The Lord is my shepherd;
I have all that I need.
He lets me rest in green meadows;
He leads me beside peaceful streams.
He renews my strength.
He guides me along right paths, bringing honor to His name.
Even when I walk through the darkest valley,
I will not be afraid, for you are close beside me.
Your rod and your staff protect and comfort me.
You prepare a feast for me in the presence of my enemies.
You honor me by anointing my head with oil.
My cup overflows with blessings.
Surely your goodness and unfailing love will pursue me all the days of
my life, and I will live in the house of the Lord forever" (Psalm 23:1-6).

(I love the 23rd Psalm from the New Living Translation. It gave me great comfort during Don's illness and continues to give me comfort in my grief.)

February 22, 2010 *Our* 43rd *month anniversary!*

"I can do everything through Christ, who gives me strength"
(Philippians 4:13).

February 23, 2010

"Teach us to realize the brevity of life, so that we may grow in wisdom"
(Psalm 90:12).

February 24, 2010

"For I am with you, and I will take care of you" (Jeremiah 1:19b).

"Wait patiently for the Lord. Be brave and courageous. Yes, wait
patiently for the Lord" (Psalm 31:14a).

(It was very difficult to wait patiently, especially during the times of seeing Don in pain, swollen with fluid, vomiting, having difficulty breathing, or waiting for a nurse or tech to help him.)

February 27, 2010

"Don't be afraid, He said, take courage! I am here!" (Mark 6:50b).

"When anxiety was great within me, Your consolation brought joy to my soul" (Psalm 94:19).

"I will answer them before they even call to Me. While they are still talking about their needs, I will go ahead and answer their prayers" (Isaiah 65:24).

March 6, 2010

"I know the Lord is always with me. I will not be shaken, for He is right beside me" (Psalm 25:5).

(The Lord helped me to know his presence continually. The Lord is ever close to us in our suffering.)

March 10, 2010

"When troubles come your way, consider it an opportunity for great joy. For you know that when your faith is tested, your endurance has a chance to grow. So let it grow, for when your endurance is fully developed, you will be perfect and complete, needing nothing" (James 1:2-4).

March 14, 2010

"We are pressed on every side by troubles, but we are not crushed. We are perplexed, but not driven to despair. We are hunted down, but never abandoned by God. We get knocked down, but not destroyed. Through suffering, our bodies continue to share in the death of Jesus so that the life of Jesus may also be seen in our bodies" (2 Corinthians 4:8-10).

March 18, 2010

"He does not ignore the cries of those who suffer" (Psalm 9:12b).

March 19, 2010

"Who can survive unless God has willed it" (Numbers 24:23).

March 28, 2010

"You keep track of all my sorrows. You have collected all my tears in Your bottle. You have recorded each one in Your book" (Psalm 56:8).

Father, I just release Don to You. You know what is best.

(Although I knew I would miss Don tremendously, I also realized that he would be in the presence of the Lord in heaven where there was no more suffering.)

(The Lord began giving me scriptures concerning sorrow and grief weeks before Don went home to be with the Lord. My precious Lord was again preparing my heart for what was to come.)

April 5, 2010

"To all who mourn…, He will give a crown of beauty for ashes, a joyous blessing instead of mourning, festive praise instead of despair" (Isaiah 61:3).

April 16, 2010

"March on with courage, my soul!" (Judges 5:21b).

April 22, 2010 Our 45th month anniversary!

"When I am overwhelmed, You alone know the way I should turn" (Psalm 142:3a).

April 29, 2010

Father, help me to keep praying with faith no matter what happens because I know that You will give the answers in Your time. You are truly trustworthy. Give me strength for this day. Thank you Lord for peace, rest, hope, assurance, and all the wonderful ways that You have of blessing me and loving me.

April 30, 2010

"I commit Don to you again, Lord."

(There were many nights when I said to the Lord, "Don's not coming home, is he?" During the day it was somehow easier to keep my emotions under control, but I couldn't at bedtime. It was very difficult to think of Don never coming home again. I was already grieving.)

(Really special times were those we spent listening to beautiful music at bedtime as we were talking and reminiscing about our day, and how much the Lord had blessed us.)

May 1, 2010

"The Lord is close to the brokenhearted; He rescues those whose spirits are crushed" (Psalm 34:18).

"Jesus Christ is the same yesterday, today, and forever" (Hebrews 13:8).

May 3, 2010

Father, Your Word is like a healing balm for my soul. Help me to live in holiness and surrender. Thank you for Your faithfulness. I exalt You and praise You. Thank you for giving me peace especially in the midst of the storm.

(Note: "…Suffering should be thought of as the necessary pain that accompanies spiritual growth.") (2 Corinthians 1:6-7)

May 13, 2010

"Weeping may remain for a night, but rejoicing comes in the morning" (Psalm 30:5).

"I have tested you in the furnace of affliction" (Isaiah 48:10).

May 18, 2010

"And the very words I have spoken to you are spirit and life" (John 10:10).

"Precious in the sight of the Lord is the death of His saints" (Psalm 116:15).

(Note: "the Lord's loved ones are precious to God, and He carefully chooses the time when they will be called into His presence.") (Psalm 116:15)

"But God will redeem my life from the grave; He will surely take me to Himself" (Psalm 49:15).

May 19, 2010

"He will wipe every tear from their eyes, and there will be no more death or sorrow or crying or pain" (Revelation 21:4).

Note: "No matter what you are going through, it's not the last word – God has written the final chapter, and it is about true fulfillment and eternal joy for those who love Him." – Revelation 21:4

Note: "Death – "It is the doorway to a new life – eternal life." –Hebrews 12:14-15

May 22, 2010 Our 46ᵗʰ month anniversary!

Don went home to be with the Lord around 7:40 a.m.

"The Lord will fulfill [His purpose] for me" (Psalm 138:8)

(I miss Don so much!)

"Your heart winces at the pain of heavy grief, but God sees the sorrow deepening and enriching your life." –From *Streams in the Desert*, by Mrs. L.B. Cowman

Malcolm J. McLeod said, "A person's character is strengthened most during the darkest days."

(Looking back over the last year, I think Don had set his sights on the reality of heaven because of the things he said and did before his final illness. I believe he knew there was not a lot of time left on earth. He read several books about heaven, and we often talked about heaven. Many times he said to me, "Remember how much I love you." Several times Don said he should probably go ahead and give his son David all the important papers. He reminded me about the life insurance he had purchased and told me to remember where I had filed it. I put it in a file without even looking at the policy the day Don handed the folder to me. When I found the folder a few days after Don's home-going, I could hardly believe what I saw. The policy was dated May 21, 2007 which was exactly three years before his home-going on May 22, 2010. My thought, he planned this, too. The policy paid the full amount after three years.)

May 25, 2010 Don's funeral service

Father, You are amazing. What could have been a very difficult day was a glorious day because of Your hand. I truly believe You were glorified.

Our Story

*M*y first memory of Don McMillan was hearing the timbre of his beautiful bass voice in choir practice. Sitting on the back row in choir practice just a few chairs apart, I am not even sure I knew his name then.

After attending another church for years, it was a surprise when Don unexpectedly showed up at First Baptist where his son David and daughter-in-law Susan were members. They didn't realize Don was even at the same church, so you can imagine their shock when he came forward for membership after the service. David and Susan were choir members which is probably why Don also joined the choir.

Before her death, Don devoted himself to caring for his wife Nell who had been diagnosed with cancer. In 2003, Nell passed away after 57 years of marriage. Following Nell's death, Don, who had always been a busy man, found himself without a purpose and facing a sense of loneliness. Initially Don sought refuge in work but a heart attack in 2004 left him feeling as though he were a burden to those who loved and cared for him.

Being single presented a new set of challenges for Don. As he didn't know his way around the kitchen, Don avoided the stove, usually warming something for himself in the microwave. Despite knowing Don was a finicky eater, his daughter-in-law Sheila (his son Mike's wife) frequently brought food to his house, and she and Mike ate with him. What Don really loved was sweets, and left to his own devices would have had them for breakfast, lunch and dinner. When she was in his kitchen, Sheila often noticed the evidence of Don's cookie suppers.

Don was also a butter lover. Often when ordering a baked potato with his steak, he asked for lots of extra butter, saying the potato was just a carrier for the butter. It was on everything, his peanut butter and jelly sandwiches or any other sandwich (on both slices of bread) for that matter. Butter was the foundation, a staple. As a young child Don's father worked for a meat company so meat was always on the table and it was something Don enjoyed throughout his life. Meat, butter and sweets: a heavenly spread in Don's book. From a description of his eating habits, one might surmise that Don was a large man. He was not. Don **said** he would eat peas and carrots, but come to think of it, that only occurred twice in the almost four years of our marriage. As Don would say, he never met a cookie he didn't like; I would say he never met a vegetable he really liked. You might say, no wonder he had a heart attack, but the man lived 84 years.

Don's first heart attack occurred in April of 2004. Home alone, uncomfortable for hours and just hoping the discomfort would go away, Don finally called an ambulance. Weakness overwhelmed him as he struggled to get out of bed to answer the door for the paramedics. Not wanting to trouble his family in the middle of the night, Don left it to the ER technicians to finally call his sons.

Once in the ER the doctors determined there was nothing more they could do for Don. Susan, his daughter-in-law, insisted that he be transported to the nearby city of Tulsa to a heart hospital specializing in caring for patients like him. It was this decision that Don credited for saving his life. Once in Tulsa, Don underwent triple-bypass surgery and although he recovered quite well from it, he was readmitted to the hospital in June with double pneumonia.

Over his long life, Don accomplished many things of which he could be very proud and gave him a sense of usefulness. His work gave him a sense of fulfillment but when health issues forced Don to leave his career behind for good, he discovered he had to learn who he was apart from the things he had done. I'd say that is true for most of us. "I am an engineer." "I am a teacher." Those statements identify a person's vocation but what a person does is not as significant as who he is in Christ. As Christians, our most important identification is "Child of God." It is the springboard to all that we do. Don came to see that his value was not in what he had accomplished in life while his health was good. He came to realize that he was valuable because God declared it so, and then gave His only Son to prove it. For a man who was used to finding his purpose in the doing, this revelation didn't come easily. Every child of God has to come to the place where he or she recognizes that self worth is not in the doing, but in the knowing; knowing Jesus, the One and only Savior. Oswald

Chambers in *My Utmost for His Highest* wrote "The most important aspect of Christianity is not the work we do, but the relationship we maintain and the surrounding influence and qualities produced by that relationship."

Don's sharing his innermost thoughts and feelings with me was something he said he had never done with anyone before. I am now sharing Don's heart to hopefully help those who may need the assurance of knowing how much God loves them and desires a relationship with them. The Lord has given life to us, but He wants us to give our lives back to Him. Jesus said, "If you try to hang on to your life, you will lose it. If you give up your life for my sake, you will save it" (Luke 9:24). God already knows everything about us, our thoughts, our pain, our sins, our desires, our hopes, and our dreams. In her book, *Streams in the Desert*, Mrs. L.B. Cowman wrote, "Trust God's Word and His power more than you trust your own feelings and experiences." And, "God often guides us through our circumstances."

Later as Don began to read God's Word and seek a deeper relationship with Christ, his outlook on life dramatically changed. In a card that he gave me for our second month anniversary he wrote, "You have changed my life from despair and loneliness to love and joy." Although I was not responsible for changing Don's life, I did share with him how God had changed my life through the every morning discipline of having a quiet time reading God's Word and spending time in prayer. There is no substitute for God's truth. Jesus said, "I am the way, the truth, and the life" (John 14:6). It is in knowing the person, the character of Christ through His Word and His Spirit within us that we experience life with true freedom and joy, and a hope filled future. Paul said, "I pray that God, the source of hope, will fill you completely with joy and peace because you trust in Him. Then you will overflow with confident hope through the power of the Holy Spirit" (Romans 15:13).

In a letter Don once wrote to me, he said, "I want to thank you for all the things you have given me, like: anxiety attacks, impatience, a rapid heartbeat, and oh yes, JOY, RENEWED ZEST FOR LIVING, AND A REASON TO CONTINUE MY RESIDENCE ON THIS EARTH!" Don's attitude had drastically changed from despair to joy because he had put his hope and trust in the Lord. That is true of every person who puts his trust in the hands of God. A life he never imagined follows. It doesn't mean it will be an easy road but it will be blessed, full of joy and peace. God has good intentions towards His children which He shared through the prophet Jeremiah. "For I know the plans I have for you," says the Lord.

"They are plans for good and not for disaster, to give you a future and a hope." "If you look for me wholeheartedly, you will find me." "I will be found by you, says the Lord" (Jeremiah 29:11; 13-14).

Death was something that had confronted Don at an early age. His mother died from leukemia when he was only seventeen. Years later, Don's father died from a heart attack at the age of 68. His sister succumbed to cancer when she was only in her fifties. Several times in his own life Don came close to death, once when he was a child, later as an older man experiencing a heart attack, and shortly thereafter when he came down with double pneumonia. That Don lived 84 years was a miracle considering his genetic predisposition and eating habits.

A new direction!

During my previous marriage, my husband's rare neurological disease required that he be placed in an assisted living facility in the fall of 2004. As his medical bills mounted, I needed an additional $400 a month so that I could pay for his fulltime care. "Your Father knows what you have need of before you ask Him" (Matthew 6:8). I shouldn't have been surprised when my need was met so quickly. Miraculously, the following Sunday night, as I sat by a woman in church, she let me know about a part time job that had become available at the Christian Life Center. What a tremendous and timely answer to my prayers. It was instances like this that taught me to trust the Lord in all things, and with all things. No doubt He had paved the way for me for I was hired the very next day! "O my people, trust in Him at all times. Pour out your heart to Him" (Psalm 61:8a). The Lord has proven himself faithful! God must have been grinning when I got that job at the CLC. Being hired by Clint Hayes, knowing that his wife was the daughter of David and Susan McMillan, little did I know, one day in the near future I'd marry Julie's grandfather, and acquire the last name "McMillan."

Our church's Wednesday evening services are held in Fellowship Hall with dinner being served before the service. Because our church was interested in attracting younger people to the Wednesday night service, our committee discussed ways to make the tables more attractive. What I thought was a tool to attract young people to a service was also the very tool the Lord used to ignite an attraction of an altogether different sort. Previously, at a family reunion, I observed how my cousin had tied napkins around the silverware using a pretty ribbon. Some of the greatest treasures God offers us are not necessarily attractive. Jesus our Savior was born in a stable and rode into Jerusalem on a donkey. God is at work in the smallest and most mundane details of our lives. "God chose things the world considers foolish in order to shame those who think they are wise" (I Corinthians 1:27).

Sitting in the control room at the CLC, I found myself with plenty of free time so I began to wrap the silverware for the Wednesday service. After my husband had passed away and I stopped working at the CLC, I continued to wrap silverware for the Wednesday night meals, but moved the process to Fellowship Hall. The senior adults met there each Monday morning to fellowship and listen to a speaker. Although I was a senior adult, I had never attended up to that time.

It was one of those mornings that a very nice, silver haired gentleman with the warmest of smiles came walking over to my table. He introduced himself to me, and asked was there something he could do to help. Who would have ever dreamed that through wrapping silverware together a deep and abiding friendship would grow between Don and me. Every Monday Don was in Fellowship Hall, having already collected all the supplies, and was steadily working when I arrived on time at 10. As the weeks went by, I discovered that one of Don's many attributes was punctuality plus, always early, never ever late.

Don's penchant for punctuality reminded me that our God is reliable, faithful. All that He does is with purpose. "For everything there is a season, a time for every activity under heaven" (Ecclesiastes 3:1). God's timing is always perfect, right on time, never early, never late, which gave me a great sense of security and trust in Him.

One day as I listened to the messages on my answering machine, I heard Don's voice telling me he wouldn't be there the coming Monday. To my shock he ended the call by saying, "I love you." He loved me? He loved me! Later Don confessed that the words just tumbled out of his mouth. I must admit that I replayed his message over and over, each time with a smile, but still telling myself I didn't want a relationship. I was convinced of that.

My daughter Shellie and I attended a Beth Moore Conference in Oklahoma City which began June 23, 2006. There, during one of our conversations, I mentioned to her that I had met a very nice man who helped me wrap silverware. Actually, I told Shellie that Don was the nicest man I had ever met. I assured her however, that I only wanted to be his friend. How was I to know that the Lord would use a Christian women's conference to dismantle my preconceived ideas, and introduce His own plans for my life.

On Friday night of the conference, Beth Moore spoke about trusting the Lord with every area of our lives: emotions, finances, relationships, etc. As we trusted God with each particular area, the enemy's fiery darts could not penetrate our hearts. She compared it to our holding up the shield of faith or trust. As Beth Moore continued, I thought over the many experiences of my life, how I had seen God at work in my life and in the lives of others close to me. I guess I honestly believed that I trusted God with everything and that He truly had all of me, but back at the hotel that night and trying to sleep, it seemed as if the Lord and I were wrestling. As Beth's words about distrust, bleeding wounds and hurts flooded my thoughts, I was losing the struggle to believe that I really did trust the Lord with every area of my life. Oh, I did have bleeding wounds. I did distrust God. In truth, I hurt! That night I was able to confess my sins and receive His forgiveness and peace. Working in His mysterious ways, the Lord opened my eyes a little bit at a time.

The conference was incredible and I came away knowing the Lord had used a petite woman from Texas to speak specifically to me. I also recognized that God had been preparing the soil of my heart for many months prior to the conference so that He could plant His words of life. Flipping back a few months in my personal journal, I was able to see that the Lord had been answering my prayers and helping me to trust Him. Oh, how I wanted to trust Him. My heart's desire was to learn to submit to His will, to surrender my life entirely to Him (including my relationships). It was all spelled out in ink on the pages of my journal.

Somewhere during the weekend of the women's conference, I realized that my heart already belonged to Don, and I did want more than just a friendship with him, but then I wasn't sure how I could make Don aware of my feelings. With so many exciting, loving, apprehensive, and even fearful thoughts warring in my head, I could hardly wait to see Don, but what I really needed was to talk to him! Could this really be me? Had God, despite my past stubbornness and unwillingness to put my entire life in His hands, now renew my hope, fill me with His joy and introduce me to love? The answer was "yes" and "amen." I not only trusted the Lord to direct my every step, but I also allowed Him to navigate my heart through those unchartered waters of new love.

After the enlightening weekend in Oklahoma City, Don and I wrapped silverware on Monday morning once again. Although there was a lot of silence that day, I finally had the courage to tell him what I had been thinking all weekend. Remembering an earlier incident that I didn't quite know how to handle, I had asked Don his opinion of the situation, but later realized that he thought I was talking about him. The silence was broken that day by my reminding Don that I had asked for his thoughts on "the situation" saying "Do you remember all that ranting and raving I did? Well, I want you to know that none of that applied to you." There was complete silence for quite awhile and then he said, "You would be very easy to love." Later Don told me he should have said, "You are very easy to love." I think we were both in shock, and certainly speechless, so we finished our work, put things away, said goodbye and left. Feeling a little deflated and wondering what would happen next, I tried to just keep trusting and waiting on the Lord, but it was difficult nevertheless.

Not wanting to admit it to ourselves, I think we both knew we already loved one another. That day was a new beginning. We talked later about how the Lord had ordained and orchestrated every circumstance in both of our lives up to that point. I had no idea what God had planned for us in the future, but I knew I could trust him with whatever it was. God had taught me that. It seems I always have had to learn the hard way.

For some reason, I went to the church the following Wednesday around noon, slipping in through the alley door of the Fellowship Hall. As I was entering, Don was exiting. Startled to run into each other, we both found ourselves at a loss for words. Neither of us had ever been down at the church at midday on Wednesdays. Reflecting back on that day, neither of us could remember why we were ever there. Nervously, Don asked me if I would go to breakfast with him the next morning, and of course I answered with a "Yes." After the fact, Don admitted having driven by my house to ensure that he knew the way. Mr. Punctuality wasn't about to be late on a first date. By the way, he arrived a little early. That there ever was a first date both thrills and astounds me to this day.

Thursday morning arrived, and Don took me to Paul's Diner where he and his sons were regulars every Saturday. It was not a fancy restaurant, but the food was great and the company even better. Don would later apologize for taking me there for a first date, but it truly never mattered to me. Scarcely eating our food, we talked on and on, the moments slipping away into familiar chatter and laughter.

Maybe two weeks later after we had finished our weekly wrapping of the silverware, Don asked if I would walk to the Chapel with him. Sitting down close to the front in a pew, Don said, "This is where I would like us to get married." And I replied, "You haven't asked me to marry you." "Well, I'm going to," he said, but I want it to be special. With his already planting the marriage thought in my head, there was no question about my acceptance. I have tried to remember when Don officially asked me "the question," but for the life of me, I can't. Many times during our marriage we talked and laughed about "goin' to the chapel, gonna get married."

You can imagine how totally shocked our children were when Don and I announced our impending marriage. You have to keep in mind that we had only just told our families about our budding interest in one another. Our announcement was followed by a family intervention of sorts, when my daughter and granddaughter confronted me when I was visiting at their home. "Mother, are you sure about this?" my daughter asked. I longed for my family to be happy for me, to understand that this was a "God thing." I didn't have to be concerned about their feelings for long, though, for once they got to know Don, they loved and embraced him.

Just as I had never planned to marry again, Don also believed he, too, would remain single. How ironic that God would put two people together who truly believed they were destined for singleness! We were given to one another by God and we knew it, but once we decided to marry, we thought maybe we should wait a while. A friend who knows and loves me much said, why wait since our relationship was orchestrated by God. She reminded me that we were not naïve kids but mature adults who heard from God. She made the point that we weren't young, that time was short and that we weren't the type of people to make reckless decisions. This one had been bathed in prayer.

When I told Don what she had said, it was all he needed to hear and he began making plans immediately. He was definitely a planner. In the quiet of the Library (Don with his pen and notepad in hand), we began to outline our ideas for the church wedding that Don thought we should have. That we had been seeing each other seriously for such a short time was no longer an issue. The wedding date was set for July 22, 2006, in the chapel, and we couldn't have been more thrilled, actually giddy with excitement. Don even made our invitations himself, putting one in each Sunday bulletin, inviting our entire church family, which was very important to Don. Both he and I wanted to involve everyone in celebrating this marvelous love we had for one another, seeing it as a gift from God. Come to think of it, several people in our church family told us they knew about our feelings for one another long before we did. Could it have been because we were always smiling?

Isn't it funny that two people can decide to get married quickly, but no matter how early the wedding date is set, it just seems to take forever to arrive? Well, July 22, 2006 finally rolled around, and what a glorious day it was when our pastor, Lance Sawyer united us in marriage.

It was a beautiful ceremony, and neither Don nor I could stop smiling. Nestled together in the chapel's pews where Don had first broached the idea of our marriage, now sat family members and friends who had come to witness our vows and share in our delight. It was a joy to share our day with them. Though we said we wanted no wedding gifts, some of my friends couldn't resist. Alluding to how Don and I met, they gifted us with wind chimes, homemade from of all things, silverware. It was the real thing, the kind I have to polish, no less.

Later I learned that Don's sons were also very shocked by our plans to marry and really didn't know what to think, but despite their concerns the whole family was very gracious, embracing me as one of their own. To this day, I thank the Lord for my McMillan family, whose hearts are forever knit with mine.

The following is a prayer from my journal just before our wedding:

"Father, I pray that Your Word would burn in our hearts like a fire. Thank you for standing beside us like a great warrior against the enemy. Help us to faithfully proclaim Your Word. Thank you for the plans you have for us, plans for our good, to give us a future and a hope, and for promising that we will find You, if we seek You with all our heart, mind, and soul. You will give back our health and heal our wounds. You love us with an everlasting love and have drawn us to You. You will walk beside us and even if we stumble, we will not fall. We will be radiant because of Your many gifts to us. Our lives will be like a well watered garden and our sorrows will be gone. You have turned our mourning into joy and given us comfort. You have exchanged our sorrow for rejoicing. You have said there is hope for our future, that if we return to You, You will restore us. You will give us rest. You will cause something new and different to happen. We will embrace You, our God. You will write your laws on our hearts and put them in our minds. You will do all the good things you have promised. You said to ask You and You would tell us some remarkable secrets. If we trust You, You will preserve our lives and keep us safe. You will build us up and not tear us down, You will plant, not uproot us. You will protect us. Help us to buckle on your full armor and advance into battle against the enemy. Help us to not be afraid or dismayed, because You are with us. You are our place of rest. Let us bind ourselves to You. You are our defender. We are Your children and Your own special possession. You are the center point of our lives and our marriage. We thank you for bringing us together, and we pray for Your guidance in all we do. Amen."

During the wedding ceremony, Pastor Lance used the example of a triangle with God at the top, Don on one of the lower corners and me on the other one. He explained that the closer we grew to God, the closer we would grow to one another. This truth not only applies to marriage partners but to the entire body of Christ, the church.

I know with certainty if we had not been seeking a closer relationship with the Lord and growing in maturity, our relationship would not have been as sweet as it was. Both of us were equally determined to grow in our relationship with the Lord, knowing that our relationship with one another would be strengthened and would flourish. I believe a strong marriage is dependent on our having a strong relationship with the Lord. The more we know about our Father's love for us and as we learn to love him, the more we can love one another. "If we love each other, God lives in us, and His love is brought to full expression in us" (1John 4:12). From the beginning, Don and I began to pray with one another. We agreed to have our private quiet time with the Lord separately, first thing every morning, before beginning our day with one another. Even on Sunday mornings we set the alarm earlier, so we could have our quiet time and still have plenty of time to get ready for church, early!

From the time Don and I first met, we never had a cross word or a disagreement. Time and energy was never wasted being angry with one another. We endeavored to reflect Christ to one another and to those in our lives, so that room was never made for the enemy to come in. We just thanked the Lord every day for bringing us together and blessing us so much. We lived gratefully, often talking about all the different circumstances that had to have come together at just the right time in order for us to even meet.

Being with Don was always a lot of fun because he had a great sense of humor. We enjoyed taking short trips with one another. In the past, Don had traveled for several years as a consultant, a lot of times in Europe, and I had traveled quite a bit, too, so long trips no longer appealed to us, with the exception of driving to Kansas City to visit with Don's family. We went to Branson a couple of times, to Carthage to the Precious Moments Chapel, to Fantastic Caverns, to a Gaither Concert in Tulsa and to the nearby town of Tahlequah for the River City Players. During our travels, Don appointed me his navigator, which became another source of much laughter. In my experience, men did not want their wives to tell them where to go, but again Don was the exception. He was a master at U-turns, and they happened on most every trip, usually more than a few times. Being his navigator and trying to explain to Don which direction he should take, I began pointing with much drama, creating laughter every time. When he would turn the wrong way, he always told me, "You didn't point." During our last trip to Branson after having lunch at a restaurant on the outskirts of town, Don took us on an adventure. Having driven full circle around the outskirts of Branson, we ended up right back at the same restaurant. We had our excursions and made some fond memories, but perhaps the most meaningful took place right in town. Every Sunday and Wednesday night after church, Don and I went to Braum's Ice Cream and Dairy Store for frozen yogurt, where we would share in our mutual addiction and laughter.

Blending families can sometimes be a difficult problem, but our families seemed to be woven together from the start. Both Don and I wanted a smooth transition, and we couldn't have been more thrilled as we witnessed our families demonstrate mutual kindnesses and respect for one another. Don was a wise and honorable man, endeavoring to gain the acceptance of my family, rather than expecting it. Tragically many parents make the mistake of demanding trust and respect. Don had it right. He knew trust and respect had to be earned, which he did. In Don's case winning the hearts of my family was easy. He was simply himself, showing kindness in his humble sort of way.

The Lord blessed me with two wonderful children, my daughter Shellie and, three years later, my son Spencer. Shellie and her husband, Bruce, are parents of three children, Brandon, Sarah, and Matthew. Spencer and his bride, Michele, also blessed me with three grandchildren, Brenda, Mary Rose, and William. I want them to know how much I love each one of them. My son-in-law Bruce and my daughter-in-law Michele are wonderful additions to our family. I love them as if they were my own. Grandchildren, well if you have them, you know what tremendous love is stockpiled in my heart for them. What a joy they are! I thank the Lord for each one of them, and I pray that each of their lives would be a reflection of Christ.

Don was always gracious to my children, and he was ready to go anytime I wanted to see them. While visiting my son's home for the first time, my grandson, William, who was only two at the time, thought Don had come to play with him. He kept telling Don, "Come to my room and play," and wouldn't take no for an answer. A kid at heart, Don was very willing, and he and William became buddies. Anytime we were with my son Spencer and his family, William was next to Don. One of my favorite pictures is of William in Don's lap. Once, Spencer had combed William's hair into a "wild do," spiked on top, and combed back on the sides. The next morning, Don came into the room where I was with his hair just like William's. He was just grinning. It was hilarious.

Before our first month anniversary, Don told me he wanted us to celebrate our anniversary every month, which we did by going to a special place for dinner and giving one another a card. Time with one another was precious to both of us, and we had the cards with endearing words to prove it. As wonderful as the love was between us, I am reminded of what Charles Spurgeon wrote in his book Look Unto Me, "No matter how pure and intense the love of an earthly husband, it is but a faint picture of the flame that burns in the heart of Jesus."

Don had given me many cards, and I treasured and saved every one of them. My first card from him was a Christmas card in 2005, soon after he began helping me with the silverware. He had written, "Thanks for allowing me to help with the napkins and flatware." When Don was in the hospital on one of our monthly anniversaries, he told me to look for an anniversary card on his desk. Knowing Don would want me to have a card on Valentine's Day, his granddaughter, Julie, bought a Valentine's card and sent it to me. Even after he had passed away, I found two more anniversary cards on his desk. As they were still in the bag, I knew he had bought several of them so he would be prepared, which was so like him. I also found all the cards I had ever given him, along with a letter I had written. It was in response to the letter Don had written me before we were married. He printed his same letter again at the end of December, 2009, added on to it again January 4, 2009, and gave it back to me just three days before he went to the hospital.

The impact of Don's life didn't just extend to family and church members. His servant's heart was apparent in the early years of his life when he became a volunteer fireman in Corning, New York, willingly placing his life on the line to help others. Later, Don ministered to inmates at a nearby prison facility through the Genesis One Organization. He facilitated a prayer ministry, pairing prayer partners in our church with prisoners behind bars. Disappointed when his health prevented him from going to the prison, Don continued the prayer partner ministry from home.

He reached out to some young boys the Lord brought into our lives, sharing God's Word with them. Don and I also had the opportunity to minister together, mentoring couples. Looking back, that might have seemed absurd, two newlyweds mentoring others who had been married much longer than the two of us, but what Don and I had was good, rock solid from the get-go and it only got better. It was our delight to share biblical principles with others, knowing how sweet the fellowship was with God, and one another, if we would but live by them.

Don had been the director of his Sunday school class at one time, but that was just one of the many ways in which he ministered. He volunteered in the Food Pantry, helped fold the Sunday bulletin or the church newsletter. In the fall, Don could be found in the Christian Life Center helping with Upward Basketball, a ministry to young girls and boys. During Vacation Bible School, Don volunteered as a crossing guard escorting children across the street. He served as a chauffeur, driving folks to church, who had no other transportation. If Don was asked to serve, his answer was, "yes," willing to do anything he was asked to do. Together, Don and I volunteered for Trinity Hospice and regularly visited several patients in long-term care.

Have you ever encountered a person whose eyes just seemed to speak for them? Don had those kind of eyes and the warmest of hearts, a servant, an educated man who gave of himself, quietly laboring under the watchful eye of the Father. Nothing Don did said, "Look at me." He never served to be seen. As a matter of fact, considering his education, accomplishments and skills, he could have self promoted but that was not who he was. Whenever there seemed to be a need, this gentle soul availed his life to be used by the Lord without any fanfare at all. Don was very active in ministry well into his eighties, in fact, up until his hospitalization January 7, 2010.

Sweet and generous, Don always thought he had to pay for everything, always reluctant to let someone else pick up the check. When learning of a need within our church family, he gave generously, never drawing attention to himself. As Don was punctual, he was faithful, his tithe always in an envelope in his pocket, ready to be placed in the offering plate every Sunday.

One of the things that made Don so attractive was the way he loved his family. He enjoyed the times we all got together in the Christian Life Center, usually after Thanksgiving and Christmas. Don often told me how much he loved his sons, David and Mike, and each member of the family. He was so proud of them. We talked about his concerns for them, and I know he prayed for them every morning and night. Sneaking up to the door of our bedroom one night, I took a picture of Don kneeling by the side of the bed praying. He never knew I took the picture. What a precious sight it was to see him there. The scripture in 3 John 4 is indicative of Don's heart "I could have no greater joy than to hear that my children live in the truth."

Though he could not remember ever telling his father that he loved him, Don made sure each of his family members knew of his love for them. Don's grandchildren, Lisa, Julie, R.J. and Amy, and his great grandchildren, Parker, Cooper, Miranda, Autumn, Toni, Tyler and Tatum were very special to him. Following Don's funeral service, Julie and Clint's son, Parker, walked up to me several times, not saying a word, but giving me a hug each time. I still receive those precious hugs when Parker sees me at church.

Knowing how Don loved and cherished me was like opening the doors to a whole new world. I experienced a refreshing sense of being sheltered, of completeness and serenity. Don protected and sheltered me, which gave me security, in which I thrived. I can honestly say that I had never known such love, that marriage could indeed be so sweet. Don's expression of his love for me was not merely with words, but in deeds as well. He was gentle, tender, gracious, complimentary, and affectionate. With never a doubt, I knew he valued and treasured me. How wonderful it would be if every husband would treat his wife as the weaker vessel. Knowing the kind of love Don had for me gave me a greater sense of God's great and unfailing love for me, and the knowledge that the Lord values and cherishes me. Our marriage thrived because love was handed back and forth all the time. What a wonderful picture for young people. God is love! Apart from knowing God's love, how can we really love one another?

He treated me as if I were fragile and might break, so there were several chores Don thought I shouldn't do around the house or in the yard. He thought it was his job to empty the dishwasher, take out the trash, do any maintenance or repairs, and get the mail. He even did his own laundry. Sometimes, knowing I would be caught, I sneaked around and did some of those things just for fun. He would act as if I were in trouble but was smiling the whole time. Don was always patient and kind even when he was teasing me. One of the things I loved about Don was his sense of humor. We laughed every day and had lots of fun together. "A cheerful heart is good medicine" (Proverbs 17:22).

Don would tell me that he needed to do his part around our home, and he didn't want to become a burden on me. Having been responsible for everything around the home for a long time, learning to share those chores with Don was not easy for me. He was aware how difficult it had been for me to care for my previous husband before his death. In his thoughtful way, Don purposely worked hard to not be a burden, although all of Heaven knows there was no possible way he could be. I could never have felt that way about him. Looking back, I'm sure there were times when Don didn't feel very well, but because he didn't want me to worry, he didn't tell me. Usually I could tell when he wasn't feeling well, but there were times when I am sure I was unaware.

Don had an appreciation for good music, often listening to classics as he worked on the computer or at his desk. As a child he took piano lessons for nine years, which no doubt helped cultivate his love for classical music. Years later, when Don sold his home, he had very few items left, but one of the last things to go was his organ. Not only was he able to float his fingers across its ivory keys, but Don also played the sousaphone, and had marched with it in the school band when he was younger. Listening to peaceful music was a part of our nightly routine, with Don considering it his duty to turn on the CD player as we prepared for bed. He introduced me to classical music and I, well, I introduced him to Bill Gaither's praise and worship DVDs, something he had never before experienced before meeting me. Watching one of the DVDs became one of our favorite things to do.

In our culture today, good manners seem to be a thing of the past. Don was the ultimate gentleman, not just to me, but to everyone. Never trying to impress others, he was genuinely courteous, thoughtful, and polite all the time. If I credited Don's manners, telling him how much I appreciated the fact that he was a gentleman, he would in turn give credit to his father saying, "That was how I was brought up." Even while he was in the hospital, Don said "Thank you" to everyone who came into his room to care for him. Even after he had been moved to ICU some of Don's nurses, who had previously cared for him, came to see him, and others asked about him when I saw them in the hall or cafeteria. After his home-going I received a card from Becky, one of Don's nurses. He had come into Becky's life a virtual stranger lying in a hospital bed, but Don left this life as her friend. If you knew Don, you were the better for it.

Having endured some serious hurts in my life, it was wonderfully sweet to live with a man like Don who always put me first, always considered my needs and desires ahead of his own. It was refreshing to hear "What do you want to do?" How do you feel about…?" In short, I mattered to him. With Don I always had a voice. Even in the small things he considered me. Even in those moments when Don was able to lean back in his chair, prop up his feet, and watch a much anticipated football game, he was still willing to change the channel. He epitomized I Corinthians 13:5, "Love does not demand its own way." As much as Don enjoyed watching football on television, he never demanded to turn the channel to a game. He always asked me if there was something I would rather watch. Most of us are selfish, wanting our own way, but Don was never like that. He was a man who had surrendered his will to God, and in doing so became a servant/husband who made me feel that I was very loved and cherished, safe and secure. Content to just be near him, I didn't much care what Don and I were doing or where we were. I just enjoyed being with him. We were best friends.

Don's general disposition matched his manners. He was as sunny as he was kind. One of the things that made Don's life such an inspiration is that he lived intentionally, moment by moment, day by day. He lived for Christ so much so that Jesus was beautifully displayed through Don to those about him. That the Spirit of God resided in Don was not only evident in his actions but also in his attitudes. If you asked Don a thousand different times in one day how he was doing, he would always respond with one word, "Wonderful." He was wonderful when he could barely breathe, when he was in pain, and when he could hardly keep anything down. "Wonderful," was just Don's way of viewing life from God's perspective. I'm sure everyone who knew him thought that he was wonderful. I know I surely did. God must have saved the best for last.

Don McMillan

Don McMillan

Our Wedding Day
July 22, 2006

One of our family gatherings at the Christian Life Center
Julie and Cooper Hayes, Tyler and Toni McMcMillan, Parker Hayes, Don,
Autumn Mix, Tatum McMillan, Miranda Horton
(Don's granddaughter Julie, and his great grandchildren)

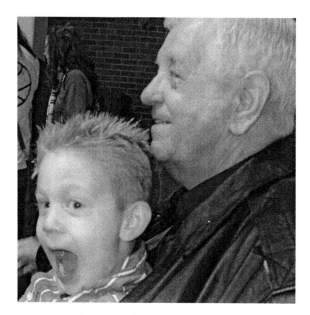

Lyndia's grandson William with Don

Don's spiked hair

Don's son, David and Susan McMillan with grandson Parker Hayes

Don's son, Mike with wife Sheila

Don's Hospitalization And Home-Going

*I*n the middle of the night on January 6, 2010 Don woke up with a fever and began vomiting. Upon awakening and realizing Don was very sick, I called his son David asking for his help in transporting Don to the emergency room. Back in January and November of 2009, Don had been hospitalized with similar symptoms. The November visit resulted in the doctors informing us that Don would need to have his gallbladder removed, but the surgery would have to wait until they could successfully treat his pneumonia.

It was round two with pneumonia, but this time Don had double pneumonia, along with a severe gallbladder attack. In the past, Don had contended with severe pain in his shoulders and had made several visits to a bone and joint clinic where he received cortisone injections. Now Don's gallbladder was discovered to be the true source of his pain.

Don's doctor chose to address the infections in Don's lungs first, which was then followed by an operation on January 20, 2010. Initially, the surgeon hoped to perform laparoscopic surgery, but because Don's gallbladder was so inflamed, the doctor was unable to do so. What seemed then to be a precarious situation turned into relief as the gallbladder surgery appeared be tolerated.

Just before the technician came to transport him to surgery, Don began praying aloud one of the most beautiful prayers I had ever heard. Praying for God's will to be done, he thanked the Lord for giving him life and blessings. Don let the Lord know that if He was so inclined to take him home, he was ready to go. Don also prayed that the Lord would be with the surgeon, guiding his hands as they were in the operating room. Including his family and me in his prayer, Don asked the Lord to grant us peace. I wish that I could remember all the words that Don uttered in prayer that day, because the prayer truly was touching. Typical of the man he was, Don's prayer was so selfless and full of concern for others.

Three days had passed since Don's gallbladder had been removed when the tide seemed to turn. Out of the blue Don started grappling with nausea and intense pain as bile began leaking into his abdomen. It was the doctor's belief that the bile would simply stop leaking, but it continued to do so. Also, Don received several blood transfusions because of low blood counts. At the time the reason for them was a mystery, but later a hematoma was discovered on his liver, caused by the inflamed gallbladder that had been pressing against it.

Because of the seriousness of Don's health and his need for more specialized care, he was transferred to St. Francis Hospital in Tulsa on January 26. After starting an Endoscopic Retrograde Cholangio-Pancreatography, a procedure in which a scope was inserted into Don's esophagus and ultimately leading into the bile duct, a stricture in the lower bile duct itself was discovered, and the doctor's were prevented from going any further. Two days later, which would have been Day 23 of his hospitalization, Don's doctors did a Percutaneous Transhepatic Colangiogram with biliary cathether drainage. This procedure allowed the bile to drain out of his abdomen. Anticipating Don would need additional blood transfusions, specialists inserted a Peripherally Intravenous Central Catheter, through which they were also able to administer the nutrition Don needed. Overall, Don had had very little to eat during his entire hospitalization, and his weight continued to drop. What little he was able to eat usually came right back up, and ultimately Don lost close to 50 pounds.

It was on Day 35 that friends from our church, Don and Sharon Hendricks, came to the hospital to visit Don. A few days later Don Hendricks returned by himself, staying for quite a while. My Don was feeling well enough to talk with him and thoroughly enjoyed their time together. They discussed the various positions my Don had held while working for different companies, along with the many interesting places my Don had gone to conduct personnel seminars. Don Hendricks was a high school football coach, which gave the two of them plenty to talk about, since my Don so enjoyed watching the sport on television. The days Don spent in the hospital were filled with physical pain, beeping monitors, a continuous flow of nursing staff and endless sticks from needles. That was our normal, which was why the lively conversation between the two Dons was so special. There amidst a sterile setting, I had the joy of listening to their warm conversation about life, the things that took place beyond the hospital walls. What a shock it was when Don Hendricks died suddenly, not long after that. Since my Don was so sick at the time, I decided not to tell him.

Day 43 rolled around, and Don began having difficulty breathing as fluid began to build up in his body. Watching Don steadily decline, I found it was a relief when the decision was made to transfer him to ICU where he would receive acute care. The day before these things took place, I had written the following verse in my journal: "When you pass through the waters, I will be with you" (Isaiah 43:2). Thinking about Don's current physical condition, that his body was retaining so much fluid, I thought the verse was very appropriate.

Up until the time Don had entered ICU, I had pretty much stayed with him in the Tulsa hospital practically every night, at times rotating shifts with family members. Once Don entered the ICU, I made the 45 mile trek back to our empty home each night, normally making the drive alone. As it often is with caregivers, there was a point at which I became very tired and somewhat numb, seeming to operate on auto pilot. Had it not been for the Holy Spirit sustaining me, I would have crumbled under the weight of it all. Deep down I felt compelled to be at Don's side. I wanted to be with him, near him. When I had to be at home, being apart from Don was almost unbearable, and I could hardly wait to get back to the hospital. My life at that point was centered on one man, the love of my life, and seeing him restored to health.

Everything except my relationship with the Lord fell by the wayside. Tucked away in my tote bag, and making the daily journey with me to the hospital, was my journal, a calendar, and most importantly, my precious Bible. The Word of God was my stay through this tumultuous time, giving me the strength and direction for each day, always preparing me for what lay ahead. You would think my journal would have been filled with all my thoughts and prayers, that I would have poured out my heart on its pages, but truth be known, at the time I was so numb I could hardly think, let alone write. What I did jot down were Bible verses the Lord gave to me during my daily quiet time, and they seemed to speak to each situation we faced. "Whenever trouble comes your way, let it be an opportunity for joy. For when your faith is tested, your endurance has a chance to grow. So let it grow, for when your endurance is fully developed, you will be strong in character and ready for anything" (James 1:2-4).

My journal and calendar became a record of physician's orders and Don's state of health. They also served as a guest registry as I noted each visitor that came to see him.

After consulting with the surgeon, we were informed Don would have to undergo another procedure, so on Day 54 of his hospital stay he underwent gastric bypass surgery. In performing this surgery, the hope was that the bile would be made to drain directly into Don's intestines, thus addressing all the problems which brought about his initial hospitalization. The doctors had deemed the surgery a success, so Don's daughter-in-law Sheila and I were alarmed the next morning when upon arriving at the hospital we learned Don's blood pressure had dropped dangerously low. Frantically we called for a nurse, who in turn called for a Crash Cart, a portable trolley containing all the equipment and drugs required for cardiopulmonary resuscitation and emergency care. As his head was tilted to the side and he wore a vacant stare, I was certain that we were losing him. Don quickly received intubation and was then placed on a ventilator, which along with medication helped to stabilize his blood pressure. Because Don's blood count was very low, doctors thought this frightening event was likely due to an internal bleed. As the nurses worked to stabilize him, a nun who actually lived at the hospital slipped into Don's room and prayed a really neat prayer with us.

That day, no doubt, the Lord sustained us all. In the midst of the commotion, I asked the Lord to just help me to trust Him no matter the outcome, knowing that His plans for His children are always perfect. Placing the matter in God's hands brought a peace to my heart that I would not have known had I not prayed. "You will keep in perfect peace all who trust in You, whose thoughts are fixed on You!" Isaiah 26:3).

That day I managed to write a prayer in my journal. "Father, I know Don is in Your care and that You know best. Help me to trust You no matter what. I am so thankful for the time You have given me with Don. You understand my feelings and know my heart, how I have always committed him to You and I am committing him to You once again. I pray Your will be done. I know he is precious to You." Nevertheless, the road of faith and trust would not be an easy one.

Later that evening I returned home, and fell into bed for some much needed sleep, but in the wee hours of the morning the phone rang, jarring me awake. As I lifted the receiver my eyes fell on the clock by my bed. It was 1:30 a.m. A staff nurse was calling to ask permission to take Don back into surgery. Sensing a special grace for the moment, I called Don's son David and his wife Susan who quickly came to get Sheila and me. In the car, bathed in silence, we seemed to fly the 45 miles to Tulsa but were unable to make it in time before Don was whisked off to surgery at 2:15. It was quiet as we all sat praying in the dark waiting room, not knowing if Don was strong enough to make it through the surgery. About an hour later Susan noticed Don's doctor walking out of the elevator in search of us. Don had made it through the surgery! The culprit had been a tiny bleeder which the doctors successfully cauterized.

It was now Day 55 and Don was still on the ventilator, but by Day 57 he was back to breathing on his own and the ventilator was removed. Knowing that Don came through the surgery, we had a renewed sense of optimism and were hopeful his health had turned the corner for the better. I wrote in my journal, "Thank you so much Father that Don is doing better." I included the scripture verse from Psalm 48:1, "How great is the Lord, and how much we should praise Him," as well as Psalm 46:1, "God is our refuge and strength, always ready to help in times of trouble."

By this time, Don had received so much pain medication that he had become very confused, making us laugh because of all the funny things he said. It was difficult understanding him, so we gave him a piece of paper and a pen. Most of what Don wrote was not legible but one note we could read had us all tickled, "Tell that nurse that I have had enough of this for today." He also wanted us to call the "manager" and the police, for what reason I am not sure.

One day Amy, Don's granddaughter, came to visit him. His voice was gravelly and hard to understand, but even so, yet with great effort, he tried to communicate something to her, but none of us could grasp what it was. All of a sudden Don loudly spelled the word "**C O O K I E S.**" We understood him perfectly then, and we all had a good laugh. We asked Don what kind of cookies he wanted and without any hesitation he said, "Chocolate chip." I should have known. Don and I hadn't been seeing each other for very long when he had told me that he never met a cookie he didn't like, but chocolate chip was his very favorite. It was even his favorite ice cream flavor.

By Day 70, in the evening, Don was transported to Meadowbrook, a long-term acute care hospital. He was highly medicated and extremely disoriented, growing more confused by the day. Each day the visits to Don at Meadowbrook grew more difficult. It pained me to see his condition deteriorate right before my eyes. Recognizing he was no longer in the hospital where he had received more attentive care, Don began to slip into a depression, which was understandable considering all that his poor body had been through. Physical therapy had been ordered for him but was too overwhelming in Don's weakened state. What was meant to be a transitional period in his recovery instead became a downward spiral. I marvel that some of life's most tender moments take place in some of the bleakest situations. It was during this stay at Meadowbrook that Don's granddaughter Amy gave him a much needed haircut, saving the clippings of his gorgeous white hair for me.

On Day 72, Don pulled out the PICC line. The following day he was found on the floor and on Day 76, he pulled out his IV. Don remained very confused and continued to contend with nausea and vomiting every time he was fed by his caregivers. Because of the snow on the roads, I couldn't get to Tulsa to see Don for two days which was difficult but I did turn my concerns over to the Lord, confessing my impatience and frustration at being house-bound.

Day 79, yet another PICC line had to be inserted. His kidneys were not functioning as they ought and fluid had begun building up in his lungs. Day 80 found Don on the floor once again and he did not wake up all day. His temperature rose and just as in times past he was placed back on oxygen. It was also determined that Don would have to be in an enclosed bed, confined for his own safety, something which was heartbreaking for me to see.

It was a Sunday when Don was transported back to St. Francis ER in Tulsa with sepsis, kidney failure, and double pneumonia. I had been sitting in Bible Study in Muskogee when I felt the Holy Spirit compelling me to go to Tulsa. I needed to leave immediately. Unable to ignore God's prompting, I got up in the middle of class and drove to the acute care hospital. Within a short time after my arrival at Don's bedside, the decision was made to transport him to St. Francis hospital ER. It was there, in the hospital ER, tired, emotionally worn and in pain, Don prayed for the Father to take him home to heaven. Clutching his hand in mine, I told Don it was okay to go home to Jesus. I would be alright. It had grown so difficult to watch the man I loved so deeply suffer so much. All I could do was concede to the Lord, to give sway to His will. Once again Don was admitted to ICU.

It was Day 83 and another PRCP procedure was performed. This time the procedure was a success or so we thought, as the doctors were able to place a stent in the leaking bile duct. After awhile Don's kidney function improved somewhat and his white blood count returned to almost normal.

The family and I, recognizing Don had been through so much, asked the physicians not to use intubation again. When we told Don that we had conveyed this to the doctors, he seemed much relieved.

Just 6 days later, Don had improved enough so that he was moved to a regular room but still continued to vomit after eating only a few bites of food. The biliary catheter was still in place. The doctors had hoped to remove it, but because the bile duct continued to leak even after a stent was put in, the doctors had to leave the biliary catheter where it was.

On Day 104, the decision was made to move Don to Broadway Manor, a nursing home facility in Muskogee. My sister Judi is a registered nurse, and it just so happened that that is where she worked so I felt a little bit better about Don having to be there. His vomiting continued and after a few days Don's urine darkened. A fever appeared which called for more antibiotics and he was again placed on oxygen.

Nine days later Don's infection still lingered on. The fight was gone from him and he spoke of "going home." To me, it seemed that everything the doctors were attempting had little or no affect on Don's condition. I was overwhelmed with physical and mental fatigue, sensing too that Don was slipping away from me. Mike, Don's son, commented that his dad seemed to be falling into a depression. I think everyone was.

The following day I showed up at Don's room with a memory foam mattress hoping to ease some of his discomfort, and his daughter-in-law Susan arrived with baked goods. At this point Don no longer had good days, but he still managed to eat one of the chocolate chip cookies that Susan had brought.

It was Day 117. When I got to Don's room, he was really sick, having difficulty breathing, and contending with a fever. Very concerned that his heartbeat was irregular and his blood pressure was low, the nurse told me she was calling an ambulance. Once again Don was transported back to the ER at St. Francis Hospital in Tulsa. David, Susan and I arrived at the hospital before the ambulance pulled in, and this time each of us doubted that Don would survive the trip. Imagine my joy when Don was wheeled in to the ER alive! The diagnosis was the same, double pneumonia, renal failure, and sepsis. With such a grave diagnosis, I had trouble understanding why Don was taken to a regular room. Had they given up on him? Was there nothing more the doctor's could do? Later, a hospitalist arrived and much to my relief he ordered Don transferred to ICU.

One morning before going to see Don I wrote in my journal, "Father, Your Word is like a healing balm for my soul. I exalt You and praise You.

Lyndia McMillan

Thank You for giving me peace even in the midst of the storm." "Surely God is my help; the Lord is the one who sustains me" (Psalms 54:4).

Day 122, surgery again! A troubling CT scan of Don's abdomen indicated something was horribly wrong and a decision was made to operate that afternoon. Just minutes before they took Don into the operating room, I told him I loved him, that I would be okay, and I assured him it would be alright for him to go home to Jesus. We had been to this mountain before more than once. In return, Don told me he loved me very much. Little did I know that it would be the last time I would ever hear those precious words. Once in the operating room, the surgeon could not find anything wrong but had it been what he thought, Don would have soon died. Don was placed back on the ventilator, no longer responsive. His entire body was now retaining fluid and his hands were so swollen that the nurses had to loosen the bands on his wrists. Don would not awaken again, except for just a moment one day.

A few days later I scribbled some verses in my journal, poignant for the times I was facing.

"Weeping may remain for a night, but rejoicing comes in the morning" (Psalm 30:5).

Sometimes the sorrows of darkness seem to last forever but we are promised morning, and with it, rejoicing.

"I have tested you in the furnace of affliction" (Isaiah 48:10). A furnace has a way of revealing the quality of a substance, bringing the impurities to the surface. During all this trying time, Don's faith did not waiver nor did it give way to complaint. His eyes were fixed on Jesus and he relished eternity with his Savior all the more. On my end, I so desired for this time of testing to result in an even more intimate relationship with the Lord, that I too, would be found faithful.

The waters we passed through were rough yet deep down I knew Don and I were not sinking. We had both placed our lives squarely in the Master's hands. Our confidence was in Him and we had been given a precious gift, peace. "Let the peace of Christ rule in your hearts" (Colossians 3:15). It was not a sometimes peace. We had it every day. Both Don and I made the decision to let the peace of God rule. We had given nothing else the authority over our hearts. As I looked over my journal entry for that day, these words leapt out at me, "The way to peace is to accept every circumstance and every trial as being straight from the hand of our loving Father; to live with Him in heavenly realms." (From *Streams in the Desert*, May 13th)

By the time day 131 unfolded, I knew Don wasn't going to get better. I even questioned why he was still here, knowing he was suffering, and knowing he wanted to be with the Lord. Everyone who knew Don well knew he would not want to remain on a ventilator. The family and I consulted with the doctors and amongst ourselves. We prayed, we cried, and agreed it was the right decision. We asked that Don be taken off the ventilator. The Hospice at St. Francis then took over, gently explaining what lay ahead.

On Day 132, Don was moved to a regular room. For a moment he opened his eyes, gently squeezing Susan's hand in response to her question. Then, once again Don drifted into a deep sleep.

For his birthday the past November, Susan had given Don a book designed with questions that when answered would become a record of his life. She had asked Don to please fill in as many answers as possible. I took the book to the hospital with me which proved to be enjoyable for many of the family members. As we read Don's self-description, we couldn't help but muster a smile: "brown face (tanned), silver hair, a smile, quick witted, joyful, not harmful, diligent, dependable, organizer, planner, likes things orderly." We decided he knew himself pretty well. That day I returned the book to Susan, knowing that his children and grandchildren would be blessed to learn all about Don.

God's way is perfect. "The Lord always keeps His promises" (Psalm 145:13). The entire family and I were in a holding pattern, watching and waiting. The Hospice nurse had told us Don's death was imminent, quite possibly that day. Life on hold is not easy for anyone, let alone for those who are awaiting the passing of a loved one, but one thing I know, God's ways are still perfect even when we don't necessarily understand His methods. Even the times that God has us watching, waiting, and powerless over our circumstances, even those times are perfect.

Three days had passed and Don's blood pressure had dropped, his breathing had become slower and more irregular. Family members began to gather together. Three of Don's four grandchildren, R. J., Amy, and Julie, were there in his hospital room, and his granddaughter Lisa, who couldn't be there, called from Houston to tell him goodbye. A clock on the wall ticked away the minutes which turned into hours. By evening Don's vital signs were about the same, so we decided we should all return home.

It was Saturday. Don had now been in the hospital 136 days. Waking up very early, I called the hospital and spoke with a nurse, who told me that Don's condition was rapidly declining. My daughter Shellie had been staying with me, kindly serving as chauffeur, driving me from Muskogee to Tulsa and back. Hurriedly, I made my way to Shellie's bedroom intending to beg her services again, planning to tell her we needed to leave right away. I was surprised to find her already awake and willing to leave almost immediately. As Shellie dressed, I placed a call to Don's son David. Both he and his wife Susan also rushed to the hospital. Sensing the urgency, Shellie drove with lightning speed to the city. As we pulled into the hospital parking lot, we were gifted with a rare find, a close parking space.

Shellie and I got to Don's room just after 7 a.m. His breathing was much slower and more irregular than it had been. David and Susan arrived just a little while later. By 7:40 a.m., as I sat at Don's bedside holding his hand, I watched Don breathe his last breath and go home to Jesus. His prayer was finally answered. For some time we all just sat in Don's room and cried. After awhile I called for a nurse who confirmed what we already knew. Don was gone from us and was now in the presence of his Lord. It was really hard to leave Don's side that day. I loved him. I loved his body, the face that wore so many smiles, and the eyes that twinkled often with mischief and delight. Having the opportunity to be with Don in his last moments was a treasure I will hold dear as long as I live and breathe, and knowing that God is in every detail of our lives, I was not surprised that Don's home-going happened to be on the day of our 46th month anniversary. Agreeing with Job, I could say, Praise the name of the Lord! "The Lord gave me what I had, and the Lord has taken it away. Praise the name of the Lord!" (Job 1:21b).

I believe the Lord gives us extra grace during times of grief, helps us to experience His comfort and nearness in a special way, and reminds us how much He cares for and loves us. I'm mindful just how the grace of God works. It is always on time, never too early, and never too late. Sometimes we consider a scenario so heartbreaking or tough that we think to ourselves, we could never get through *that*. We can, by God's grace, we can. We can know with a certainty that grace will be there when we need it, measured according to the size of our problem…and then some.

Grace not only gives us the ability to get through the painfully tough times, it enables us to be grateful for them. Grace has a way of bringing value and purpose to suffering that otherwise would be meaningless, and result in our bitterness. Even now I am still thanking my Lord every day for the privilege of knowing and being the wife of Don McMillan. He brought so much joy to my life, and it is God's grace that enables me to go on living without him.

My prayer the day of Don's home-going: "Father, I thank you again for bringing Don into my life, knowing that it was You who gave us such special, sweet blessings. Thank you for teaching me about relationship and love. You know that I had committed Don to You; he was only on loan. You are awesome, Lord. Thank you for preparing me for this day, for grace. You chose the time when Don went home. Thank you, Father, that You carried him all the way from the beginning to his home-going. Thank you for our sweet times together. We laughed a lot. We enjoyed one another in everyday things and celebrated Your bringing us together. Don was undoubtedly the sweetest, nicest man on earth, in my opinion. I was blessed to even know him."

Scriptures

We posted scriptures on the walls in large print for Don to read. Every time he was moved to a different room or facility, the scripture postings went, too. Sometimes it was Don who reminded us to take them. Don was also surrounded with family pictures, a constant reminder to him of how very much he was loved. Both the scriptures and the family pictures invited a lot of comments from visitors and hospital staff. Some liked the scriptures they read so much they took notes. Once, Don's respiratory therapist came into his room and said, "It is so good to see the light in this room." At first I didn't know what he meant, but the therapist explained that the light he spoke of was the light that comes from God's Word. In writing out those scriptures for Don, we were certain they would be an encouragement to him. Little did we realize at the time that they would become a source of strength and comfort to us who kept vigil over Don. God's Word was our assurance that He was right there.

"He gives power to the weak and strength to the powerless" (Isaiah 40:29).

"Always be joyful. Keep on praying, No matter what happens, always be thankful, for this is God's will for you who belong to Christ Jesus" (I Thessalonians 5:16-18).

"My gracious favor is all you need. My power works best in your weakness" (2 Corinthians 12:9).

"The Lord gives his people strength. The Lord blesses them with peace" (Psalm 29:11).

"He gives power to those who are tired and worn out; He offers strength to the weak" (Isaiah 40:29).

"When doubts filled my mind, your comfort gave me renewed hope and cheer" (Psalm 94:19).

"God arms me with strength; He has made my way safe" (Psalm 18:32).

"For the Lord has comforted His people and will have compassion on them in their suffering" (Isaiah 49:13b).

"The Lord hears His people when they call to Him for help" (Psalm 34:17a).

"Oh Lord my God, I cried to You for help, and You restored my health" (Psalm 30:2).

"But You, O Lord, are a shield around me; You are my glory, the One who holds my head high" (Psalm 3:3).

"I will praise the Lord at all times" (Psalm 34:1a).

"Be still in the presence of the Lord, and wait patiently for Him to act" (Psalm 37:7).

"The faithful love of the Lord never ends! His mercies never cease. Great is His faithfulness; His mercies begin afresh each morning" (Lamentations 3:22-23).

"LORD, there is no one like You! For You are great, and Your name is full of power" (Jeremiah 10:6).

"Don't worry about anything; instead, pray about everything. Tell God what you need, and thank Him for all He has done. Then you will experience God's peace… His peace will guard your hearts and minds as you live in Christ Jesus" (Philippians 4:6-7).

"I have learned the secret of living in every situation. For I can do everything through Christ, who gives me strength" (Philippians 4:13).

"Fix your thoughts on what is true, and honorable, and right, and pure, and lovely, and admirable. Think about things that are excellent and worthy of praise" (Philippians 4:8).

"Forget the former things; do not dwell on the past. See, I am doing a new thing!" (Isaiah 43:18).

From Life Application Study Bible, New Living Translation, Tyndale House Publishers, Inc.

Grief Intermingled With Joy

A sense of calmness, a holy peace seemed to hover over me during the last week of Don's life. I was keenly aware of the presence of God at all times, but particularly in the night hours when I was home alone with my thoughts and memories. It was in that time that the Lord graciously provided me with all that I needed, even when I was unaware of what my needs were. Over and over the Lord reminded me that I wasn't really alone, despite the fact that Don was no longer with me. God made it clear that He still had a purpose for me, and often used the life Don and I had together as a teaching tool. Even to this day, friends who know me comment that they are amazed at how well I have handled going through Don's sickness and home-going. All I can say is that I didn't handle anything. The Lord carried me through then and is carrying me still. His manifold grace has been my stay. I learned early-on in this journey to give God every detail of my life, the fears, the hurts, and even the unknown. I could only thank the Lord for all the precious memories Don and I developed in the last four years, and my heart was bent on praising God for His help and comfort.

I marvel how our spiritual gifts can keep on ministering even once we go home to be with the Father. Don had the gift of organization, and true to his gift he planned for his home-going well before his death. He made things much simpler for me because he had written out his living will and appointed his son David the overseer of his trust. Things Don would have wanted family members to have in the event of his death were given to them while he was still alive. Needless to say, because Don was organized and thoughtful, his consideration ministered to me in my time of grief. It was the way he wanted it. I believe Don loved me more than he loved himself.

Upon returning to Muskogee on Saturday, family members met at the home Don and I had lived in together. Gary Rodgers, a personal friend and director of the funeral home we decided to use, helped us plan for Don's funeral service. Don Jones, our associate pastor, who would officiate, also joined us. It was decided that David's son-in-law Clint would read the obituary. A viewing was planned for Monday from 4 to 8 p.m., with the service itself being on Tuesday morning. Surrounded by family and friends, I felt the compassion of the Lord wrap around me like a winter coat. How do people go through these times without knowing the Lord? Only He can bring the sweetness of hope and peace to a troubled soul who grapples with the death of a loved one.

The afternoon of the viewing was a tapestry of God moments. Initially I didn't think I would be able to get through it because Don's casket was stationed in the church parlor, the very place we had our wedding reception, the place I would go each Sunday morning for Bible study. True to His nature, God supplied me with an abundance of peace and graced my face with a smile. That day the mood in the parlor was light and sweet, almost celebratory in tone. How marvelous our God to do above all that we ask or think!

Don was well respected and much loved, which was reflected in the attendance of both the viewing and funeral service. Many friends and relatives filed past his casket to pay their last respects and honor the man that had lived the life of Christ before their eyes. Don was placed in a crypt on May 25, 2010. My journal entry for that day read, "Father, You are amazing. What could have been a very difficult day was a glorious day because of Your hand in all of it. I truly believe You were glorified."

There was comfort in knowing how many friends not only loved Don, but they loved me, as well. "The Lord is my shepherd; I have all that I need. He lets me rest in green meadows; He leads me beside peaceful streams. He renews my strength. He guides me along right paths, bringing honor to His name. Even When I walk through the darkest valley, I will not be afraid, for You are close beside me. You prepare a feast for me in the presence of my enemies. You honor me by anointing my head with oil. My cup overflows with blessings. Surely Your goodness and unfailing love will pursue me all the days of my life, and I will live in the house of the Lord forever" (Psalm 23:1-6).

While Don was in the hospital, Lonnie Weese, the pastor of First Christian Church in Miami, where my daughter and her family attend, came to visit at least three or four times. Pastor Weese drove an hour and a half to Tulsa to minister to all of us when Don was at St. Francis Hospital, even driving down to Muskogee when Don was hospitalized at Muskogee Regional Hospital. After driving to Muskogee for Don's funeral service, Pastor Weese lingered to talk to our Associate Pastor Don Jones. Moved by the service, Pastor Weese expressed his desire to use Don's journal in one of his sermons, so I sent him a copy.

Lonnie Weese wasn't the only one who was touched by Don's journal. Many others told me how they were impacted by his entries. What Don wrote was real and from his heart. His struggles were described honestly, and ended with him giving God the glory and praise.

A few weeks following Don's funeral, Pastor Weese arranged a special service one Sunday evening in honor of those who had passed away in the last few months, and he asked my son-in-law Bruce to talk about Don. Believing that everything happens for a reason, Bruce said he knew that God had brought Don into all our lives, using Don to make a difference in his own life.

One of the things Bruce mentioned was what an incredibly great listener Don was, having an uncanny knack of making everyone in his presence feel at ease, comfortable in their own skin. Don was the kind of man that endeavored to make all who crossed his path to feel as though they were special and important.

Don's life taught those of us who knew him that simply listening to one another is important. How could we bear one another's burdens if we didn't take the time to discover what's in their hearts?

Bruce also brought up how Don was a fine judge of character, able to read people like a book, able to know them by the words they chose to speak. Don truly practiced the art of discerning a person's character by observing facial expressions, just studying their body language in general. Little did I know there was a precise name for Don's ability, something I didn't discover until five months after his death. One day when I was searching for a definition in Don's New World Dictionary, I saw that one word in particular had been underlined. Sure that Don had been the one who had underlined the word I was made absolutely certain when I read its definition. "*Physiognomy:* one who knows < 1. The practice of trying to judge character and mental qualities by observation of bodily, esp. facial, features. 2. facial features and expression, esp. as supposedly indicative of character; the face. 3. Apparent characteristics; outward appearance."

I had to laugh. A picture of Don's face should have been right next to the definition. Don certainly did know people. His many years as a personnel manager served only to sharpen that skill. He listened to people as they spoke, studying them like a book, but no one ever left his presence feeling as though he or she was under his microscope. Don studied people, not so he could pick them apart, but so he could know them, so he could help put them back together, because he genuinely cared about them.

I attended the service in Miami that evening with my dear friend Becky, and it was on the way home that we were blessed to see the handiwork of God. There, arching against a vivid blue sky were two beautiful rainbows, their colors so brilliant and seemingly so close to us. Sensing God's presence, I was made aware yet again of His immeasurable greatness around me, His rainbows a reminder of His enduring faithfulness. The sun was shining, radiating a beauty that will forever be painted in my mind.

According to Johnny Derouen, rainbows and sunshine are only whispers of God's beauty. I agree. They are only whispers. Through His beautiful creation, God is telling us He always keeps His promises. Don loved sunny days, feeling the warmth of the sun's rays on his face. Once I peeked out the kitchen window on a summer's day to see him sitting in a chair, his eyes closed and basking in the sunlight. The brilliant rays were but a foretaste of what Don would one day experience in heaven, surrounded by the glory of his Savior. "His glory towers over the earth and heaven!" (Psalm 148:13). "The One sitting on the throne was as brilliant as gemstones... "And the glow of an emerald circled His throne like a rainbow" (Revelation 4:3). How enthralled with God's beauty Don must be. It warms me just thinking about it. Heaven is described in Revelation 21:23 as "the glory of God illuminates the city, and the Lamb is its light."

God has given me many friends, a church family, brothers and sisters in Christ that are very caring. There were those who were faithful to call, those who sent cards and encouraging notes, and those who were continually praying for me. How blessed I am! Many of them sent their condolences through providing Gideon Bibles in memory of Don, or giving contributions to the Youth Programs of our church.

I was very humbled as I read **Don's journal** once again the morning after his funeral. I just praised the Lord for allowing me the privilege of being a part of Don's life. I could see how the Lord had used this special man to help me grow in confidence. Through the power of the Holy Spirit, I began to step out in faith, sharing the Word with others, and in turn I was able to encourage Don in his relationship with the Lord. He learned to love God's Word and read it every day, jotting down meaningful scriptures on the pages of his journal.

The Lord used Don to help me overcome my shyness, which meant leaving my insecurities behind, and relying more on His Spirit. "For God has not given us a spirit of fear and timidity, but of power, love, and self-discipline" (2 Timothy1:7). God helped to grow each of us in the way He knew we needed to grow. "Two are better than one." It's true. When you have two people daily encouraging one another in the faith, it doesn't get any better than that!

When reading *Grace in Thine Eyes* by Liz Curtis Higgs, I found two profound statements from her book: the first, "Tis a long journey, grieving," and the second, "Never apologize for tears. They are so precious to God. He stores them in a bottle for safe keeping, a very large bottle."

I began thinking about my own tears, how they now arrive when I least expect them. I am unable to stop their flow. Tears of loss are mingled with joy as I reflect on all the sweet memories of my life with Don. As the salty drops roll down my cheeks, I'm very aware that my Lord has great compassion for me and is acquainted with the grief in my heart. God understands me. My finite mind cannot comprehend the Lord's ways, but I don't have to understand, just trust!

Sometimes my thoughts remind me of a delicate butterfly, flitting from one place to another. When thinking about my Creator, I know I would not exist but for Him. He knew me before the world began, when I was still in the womb, and He knows me now. He gave me the breath of life when I was born. He made all the intricate parts of my body, my spirit, and my soul. Feeling very humbled, I realize that apart from the One who stabilizes me, I am nothing. Because of Christ, I am His child, my life has purpose, and I can endure all things through Christ who strengthens me. He is already preparing a place for me where I will dwell with Him forever. He is awesome!

Heaven has been in my thoughts quite frequently and I can't help but wonder at the things Don must be experiencing. He has to be in absolute awe! It just warms my heart that Don now knows the Lord as intimately as the Lord has always known him. What must it be like to be in the Holy City with Christ Jesus, our inheritance? How must it feel to be face to face with God Himself? Is Don enjoying a family reunion? Was he welcomed at Heaven's gates by friends on earth, who preceded him in death? Is everyone dancing with joy?

Surely the music of heaven will be more beautiful than any we have heard on earth. All of paradise will be more magnificent, more glorious than we can imagine. From earth we've only but a glimpse of God's glory and beauty displayed in the splendor of a sunrise, a sunset, a vivid rainbow, a magnificent glacier calving, or a majestic snowcapped mountain. All God's wondrous creation speaks of His glory, yet all the earth and all the heavens can scarce contain it.

Someday I'll have all of the answers to my questions, but for now my thoughts continue to wander. How do people go through grief and loneliness without knowing Christ? They would have no hope, peace, comfort, or joy, only bitterness, sorrow, pain, and anger, with no promise of heaven.

I've come to discover that grief has no established pattern. The only thing predictable about grief is its unpredictability, its uniqueness to the individual. In my sorrow, I am thankful the Lord has granted me the gift of peace, tremendous comfort, and precious hope in Him. Having Christ's presence, the privilege of prayer, as well as God's grace, has been a healing balm. Though I find myself single again, I am not alone. It's quiet in the house with Don gone, but I have sweet communion with my Savior, and when the sorrow swells, it does not overtake the banks of my heart and mind. His grace always sees me through.

The journey of grief may last a long time, but I know this, I won't be traveling alone. The Lord will walk with me or carry me, all the way. Madame Guyon said, "I have learned to love the darkness of sorrow, for it is there I see the brightness of God's face." In her book, *Streams in the Desert*, L.B. Cowman says, "There are many blessings we will never obtain if we are unwilling to accept and endure suffering. There are certain joys that can come to us only through sorrow." Even the joy of our salvation came through suffering, through Christ's death upon the cross. The result of His misery and anguish is the immeasurable gift of eternal life with Him. My Father knows the sorrow in my heart and how very much I miss Don, but what God gave me by bringing Don into my life was so special and sweet, none of that is lost. Facing life without Don is not easy, but because of the living Christ in me, I will face life with joy, peace, and hope, knowing my heavenly Father is watching over me, caring for me in a way no one else ever could.

My life continues to be so much the richer because of what the Lord has done, orchestrating circumstances that continue to point me to Him.

Being with Don was a little bit of heaven on earth. I don't know why God blessed me so, but I will be forever grateful. The wonderful memories Don and I shared will be mine until I join him in heaven. I look forward to that wonderful day when I, too, will stand before Christ Jesus, my Lord and my Savior, finally home. Revelation 21:4 tells me, "He will wipe away every one of my tears. There will be no more death or sorrow, no crying or pain. These things will be done away with forever."

See you in heaven!

The Journal Of Donald David Mcmillan

July 19, 2006

"God educates us by means of people who are a little better than we are, not intellectually but 'holier,' until we get under the domination of the Lord himself, and then the whole attitude of the life is one of obedience to Him." – *My Utmost for His Highest*, Oswald Chambers

"And so I tell you, keep on asking, and you will receive what you ask for. Keep on seeking, and you will find. Keep on knocking, and the door will be opened to you. For every one who asks receives. Everyone who seeks, finds. And to everyone who knocks, the door will be opened" (Luke 11:9-10).

"Jesus replied, 'But even more blessed are all who hear the word of God, and put it into practice'" (Luke 11:28).

"If the master returns and finds that the servant has done a good job, there will be a reward" (Luke 12:43).

"For those who exalt themselves will be humbled; and those who humble themselves will be exalted" (Luke 14:11).

July 21, 2006

"Serve the Lord with reverent fear, and rejoice with trembling" (Psalm 2:11).

"In peace I will lie down and sleep; for you alone, O Lord, will keep me safe" (Psalm 4:8).

"The Lord is a shelter for the oppressed, a refuge in times of trouble. Those who know Your name trust in You, for You, O Lord, do not abandon those who search for You" (Psalm 9:9-10).

"For the righteous Lord loves justice. The virtuous will see His face" (Psalm 11:7).

""I will sing to the Lord; because He is good to me" (Psalm 13:6).

"You will show me the way of life; granting me the joy of Your presence and the pleasures of living with You forever" (Psalm 16:11).

"How can I know all the sins lurking in my heart? Cleanse me from these hidden faults. Keep your servant from deliberate sins! Don't let them control me. Then I will be free of guilt and innocent of great sin. May the words of my mouth and the meditation of my heart, be pleasing to You, O LORD, my rock and my redeemer" (Psalm 19:12-14).

"Show me the right path, O Lord; point out the road for me to follow. Lead me by Your truth and teach me, for You are the God who saves me. All day long I put my hope in You" (Psalm 25:4-5).

"The Lord is good and does what is right; He shows the proper path to those who go astray. He leads the humble in doing right, teaching them his way" (Psalm 25:8-9).

"For the honor of Your name, O LORD, forgive my many, many sins" (Psalm 25:11).

July 22, 2006

Today is my wedding day! Lord, you have blessed me every day of my life, but never so greatly, never so sweetly, as You are blessing me now. As my love for Lyndia grows each day, so does my love for You. You have awakened our capacity for romantic love, and we have expanded our capacity for spiritual love for You and our Savior Jesus Christ. Lyndia and I gratefully acknowledge Your role in bringing us together. We believe You ordained our relationship long before we recognized it… Father, we have vowed to each other that you will be the center point of our marriage. Our days will begin with our individual quiet time with You. Then we will join to worship You together, praising You for bringing us together, for renewing our lives, and for orchestrating our marriage. My hand shakes now as I contemplate the literal bliss ahead. I love You Father. I pray You will grant me many years of joy and complete commitment to my darling Lyndia, and joy and complete commitment to You, my God. Amen.

July 25, 2006

I can finally put away my anger and disbelief. I believe Jesus said if a divorced person married again, both the divorced person and the new spouse commit adultery. But, I also believe Jesus repeatedly offered forgiveness to all sinners if they accept Jesus as their Savior. Six biblical references to adultery, but forty-two references to forgiveness, provides a preponderance of evidence that Lyndia and I are forgiven, that our faith and good works have earned our right to hold our heads high. The good wishes from our Christian friends provide more evidence of forgiveness and acceptance of our pure love for each other within the framework of our love of Christ.

We are married in the eyes of God! We believe it was God who brought us together. We fell in love in God's house. We worship God individually and together. We come into His presence daily.

We are married.

We are forgiven.

We are blessed.

We begin a new life, with a clean slate, with a dedication of our lives and love to our Lord and Savior, Jesus Christ.

Who on earth can challenge this. Amen.

July 26, 2006

"Listen to my prayer for mercy as I cry out to You for help, as I lift my hands toward Your holy sanctuary" (Psalm 28:2).

"Praise the LORD, for He has heard my cry for mercy" (Psalm 28:6).

I must learn to trust Him more. I have this attitude/belief that I must take charge… I must do everything possible to help me, to protect me, to exert all that I have before I call on the LORD for help. Now, a married man once again, I must redouble <u>my</u> efforts to protect her, care for her and provide for her. To do less than that, I am being irresponsible and shirking my duty. Help me LORD, to trust You, Your wisdom, and Your strength. I want only the best of everything for her. How can I turn over to someone else my responsibility for her safekeeping? LORD, help me to trust You completely, to <u>know</u> in my heart You can and will take care of her and me, far better than I can.

Intellectually, I know You are almighty and powerful beyond measure. I believe all that the Bible says about You. But, does that authorize me to seemingly abandon my responsibility? I don't doubt Your power or Your love. I love You.

In my heart, I know You will protect her and care for her better than I can. But, in that same heart, I love her, I promised to take care of her. LORD, show me, teach me that You love her too, and You can give her better care than I can…and the best thing I can give her is my assurance that I love my LORD, I trust my LORD, and I hand over to You the care and protection of both of us. So be it! Amen.

July 27, 2006

"Jesus spoke to the people once more and said, 'I am the light of the world. If you follow me, you won't have to walk in darkness, because you will have the light that leads to life'" (John 8:12).

"You are truly My disciples if you remain faithful to My teachings. And you will know the truth, and the truth will set you free" (John 8:31b-32).

Search me, O God. Identify my sins that I might be made clean. I want to repent, I want to receive Your forgiveness, I want to be worthy of Your love and Your blessings. Wash me in the blood of Jesus, my LORD and my Redeemer. May the words of my mouth and the meditations of my heart be acceptable in Thy sight. Dear God, please continue to bless this marriage, this house, my dear Lyndia, and me. Help me to continue to learn, to grow, to commit myself to Your will. Father, help me to find that line between my husbandly duties and my trust in You. Help me to learn when to give myself to Lyndia, and when I give myself, my will, my life to You. Amen.

July 28, 2006

It is the process, not some distant result. It is the daily process of believing, trust, and obedience to God's purpose. He isn't preparing me to achieve some goal or success of my design. Daily obedience, constant worship, total absolute trust is His purpose and goal.

The Ten Commandments supports this; obedience, faith, and trust. Long ago, I accepted the Ten Commandments as my guide. I was not always obedient, but I knew the "standards" against which I would be judged. I never doubted the all-powerful God was at the heart of life on earth and in Heaven. But, TRUST, letting God lead me, submitting to His plans and decisions just didn't fit with my characterization of my role, even as a teenager, and certainly as an adult, worse as a husband. "God help me" in my mind, was a last minute, desperate plea for help AFTER all of my efforts were exhausted. To do less was an abandonment of my responsibilities. God help me, indeed, help me to throw off this self-imposed burden; this idea that I could, and should, solve every problem, make every plan and decision, that I was the sole guardian of my life and the lives of those I love. God help me to submit my will to Yours. God help me to trust You FIRST AND ALWAYS, and to accept my own ineptitude as a planner, problem solver, and protector of my loved ones. The <u>Eleventh</u> Commandment must be "Trust God with my whole heart and soul, and simply follow His lead." God help me, please. Amen.

July 29, 2006

"Wait patiently for the LORD. Be brave and courageous. Yes, wait patiently for the LORD" (Psalm 27:14).

"Praise the Lord! For He has heard my cry for mercy. The Lord is my strength and my shield. I trust Him with all my heart. He helps me, and my heart is filled with joy. I burst out in songs of thanksgiving" (Psalm 28:6-7).

"Sing to the LORD, all you godly ones! Praise His holy name. For His anger lasts only a moment, but His favor lasts a lifetime. Weeping may last through the night, but joy comes with the morning" (Psalm 30:4-5).

July 31, 2006

"For you know that when your faith is tested, your endurance has a chance to grow. So let it grow, for when your endurance is fully developed, you will be perfect and complete, needing nothing" (James 1:3-4).

Dear God, I am learning to trust You in <u>all</u> things. I know You will not fail me, whereas my plans and decisions often fail me. You have given me Lyndia. She trusts You. Lord, I pray prayers of thanksgiving and joy for Lyndia. I am so grateful that Your blessings on me need not be commensurate with my feeble attempts to serve You. I thank

You for the new opportunities Lyndia has invited me to participate in. I lose my concerns as I pray for others.

I am disposing of most of my "stuff" as I prepare for the sale of the house that has been my home for the past 23 years. A year ago, I left the church where I had been a member for (1959-2005) 46 years. That change brought me to First Baptist Church, with David and his family, to several volunteer opportunities to serve the Lord, and to Lyndia, the love of my life.

I pray relinquishing my home will lead me to even more joy, peace, and greater relationship with my Lord.

August 1, 2006

"Be still in the presence of the Lord, and wait patiently for Him to act"
(Psalm 37:7).

Last night Lyndia told me about "The fruit of the Spirit." I did not know what that was. This morning she has given me a note, quoting scripture.

"But the Holy Spirit produces this kind of fruit in our lives: LOVE, JOY, PEACE, PATIENCE, KINDNESS, GOODNESS, FAITHFULNESS, GENTLENESS, and SELF-CONTROL" (Galatians 5:22-23).

"Don't copy the behavior and customs of this world; but let God transform you into a new person by changing the way you think. Then you will learn to know God's will for you, which is good and pleasing and perfect"
(Romans 12:2).

Help me to understand how God's will and my will can clash, or combine. I want to submit completely to His will, and yet do and be what husbands are expected to be and do. Last night, I was led to understand that God will counsel and advise me. He will show me how to be a good husband, a good Christian, if I allow Him to lead me to become a good husband and a good Christian. I will love, provide for, protect, and do all that a good husband and a good Christian does, BUT God will show me HOW. Praise God!

What a revelation! I can do all those things Lyndia needs from a man; I can provide all of Lyndia's needs and desires, if I seek God and His will in all things. I have been trying to do all this ALONE. How foolish I have been. How fortunate God gave me Lyndia to lead me to the help that has been there all my life. I am not alone anymore.

August 2, 2006

"Oh, the joys of those who trust the Lord, who have no confidence in the proud or in those who worship idols. O Lord my God, you have performed many wonders for us. Your plans for us are too numerous to list. You have no equal" (Psalm 40:4-5).

August 4, 2006

Some days, LORD, you speak to me loudly. Some days, my heart doesn't resonate to what I have read or prayed. Perhaps, I am not really listening to the LORD, or even to my own voice as I read and pray. Today, however, God is speaking through Matthew 11:28.

"Come to Me all of you who are weary and carry heavy burdens, and I will give you rest" (Matthew 11:28).

"For my yoke is easy to bear, and the burden I give you is light" Matthew 11:30).

For days, I have been struggling to stop taking the lead away from Jesus, to make all my plans and decisions on my own (in a vacuum as I see it now) without allowing the LORD to take charge of my life. Looking back at my notes I see frequent references to "struggling." Dear LORD, I have stumbled upon this scripture this morning that holds the key for me. LORD, I surrender now. I submit myself, my will, my belief in my own skills, and turn to You. Where I was struggling, I now see I was struggling to retain exactly what I claimed to be releasing, what once seemed difficult, I now see as easy. LORD, I think I have it now. I still have to speak the decision; I still have to lay out the plan; I still have to take the action; BUT, I ask You LORD for Your guidance, Your advice, Your will. Oh, LORD, forgive my density and foolishness. I thank You for Your wisdom that You so graciously lay in my hands. Help me to always give You the credit, the Glory, and the Honor for all that You place at my disposal. Praise the LORD!

August 7, 2006

"For the Lord God is our sun and shield. He gives us grace and glory. The Lord will withhold no good thing from those who do what is right. O Lord of Heaven's Armies, what joy for those who trust in You" (Psalm 84:11-12).

"Those who live in the shelter of the most High will find rest in the shadow of the Almighty" (Psalm 91:1-2).

"But the godly will flourish like palm trees, and grow strong like the cedar trees of Lebanon. For they are transplanted into the Lord's own house. They flourish in the courts of our God. <u>Even in old age</u> they will still produce fruit; they will remain vital and green. They will declare, 'The Lord is just! He is my rock! There is nothing but goodness in Him!'" (Psalm 92:12-15).

Lord, let the fruit in this, my old age, be found in the hearts and minds of those for whom I pray, demonstrated in the behaviors of those who would imitate my ways. Let my old age be a fount of wisdom and rightful interpretation of all I have witnessed. Help me to give freely to all who would listen. Amen.

August 13, 2006

"But if we are living in the light, as God is in the light, then we have fellowship with each other, and the blood of Jesus, his Son cleanses us from all sin" (I John 1:6-7).

August 14, 2006

"Now may the God of peace make you holy in every way, and may your whole spirit and soul and body be kept blameless until our LORD Jesus Christ comes again" (I Thessalonians 5:23).

Lord Jesus, sanctify me. Make me clean in spirit and in my heart and mind. I plead for awareness of any and every unrepentant sin; guide me Holy Spirit to be honest with myself and my Lord, so that I can/will repent and ask Him to wash away those blemishes from my soul. Amen.

August 15, 2006

"He has saved me from death, my eyes from tears, and my feet from stumbling. And so I walk in the LORD's presence as I live here on earth" (Psalm 116:8-9).

"Those who worship false gods turn their backs on all God's mercies. But I will offer sacrifices to You with songs of praise, and I will fulfill all my vows. For my salvation comes from the LORD alone" (Jonah 2:8-9).

August 16, 2006

Jesus, Lord Jesus; come into my heart and my soul. Fill me to overflowing with Your love and the Holy Spirit. Lord Jesus, I need You and want You. Amen.

August 17, 2006

"Search me, O God, and know my heart, try me and know my anxious thoughts. Point out anything in me that offends You, and lead me in the path of everlasting life" (Psalm 139:23-24).

August 19, 2006

"We can make our plans, but the Lord determines our steps" (Proverbs 16:9).

"The man who finds a wife finds a treasure, and he receives favor from the Lord" (Proverbs 18:22).

"Enthusiasm without knowledge is no good; haste makes mistakes" (Proverbs19:2).

August 25, 2006

"Oh, that we might know the LORD! Let us press on to know Him. He will respond to us as surely as the arrival of dawn or the coming of rains in early spring" (Hosea 6:3).

It is raining this morning.

August 26, 2006

"Can all your worries add a single moment to your life?" (Matthew 6:27).

"So don't worry about these things, saying, 'What will we eat?' 'What will we drink?' 'What will we wear?' These things dominate the thoughts of unbelievers, but your heavenly Father already knows all your needs" (Matthew 6:31-32).

August 28, 2006

"If you love your father or mother more than you love Me, you are not worthy of being Mine; or if you love your son or daughter more than

me, you are not worthy of being Mine. If you refuse to take up your cross and follow Me, you are not worthy of being Mine. If you cling to your life, you will lose it; but if you give up your life for Me, you will find it" (Matthew 10:37-39).

August 29, 2006

I have just read the book of Matthew again. I am moved by the account of Jesus' ministry. It is a compelling story. It is a convincing story of God's love for mankind. It is a stark contrast with much of the Old Testament, changing from violence and wrath to love and forgiveness. I believe God is capable of both the Old Testament vindictiveness and the New Testament promises of hope and salvation. I personally, and for all those I love, want salvation. I pray now for us all.

September 5, 2006

"If you confess with your mouth that Jesus is Lord and believe in your heart that God raised him from the dead, you will be saved. For it is by believing in your heart that you are made right with God, and it is by confessing with your mouth that you are saved" (Romans 10:9-10).

September 14, 2006

"Since we are receiving a Kingdom that is unshakable, let us be thankful and please God by worshiping Him with holy fear and awe" (Hebrews 12:28).

"Remember those in prison, as if you were there yourself. Remember also those being mistreated, as if you felt their pain in your own bodies" (Hebrews 13:3).

"Therefore, let us offer through Jesus a continual sacrifice of praise to God, proclaiming our allegiance to His name. And don't forget to do good and to share with those in need. These are the sacrifices that please God. Obey your spiritual leaders, and do what they say. Their work is to watch over your souls, and they are accountable to God. Give them reason to do this with joy and not with sorrow. That would certainly not be for your benefit" (Hebrews 13:15-17).

September 17, 2006

"But you are not like that, for you are a chosen people. You are royal priests, a holy nation, God's very own possession. As a result, you can show others the goodness of God, for He called you out of the darkness into His wonderful light" (I Peter 2:9).

September 19, 2006

"Look! I stand at the door and knock. If you hear My voice and open the door, I will come in, and we will share a meal together as friends" (Revelation 3:20).

"You are worthy, O Lord our God, to receive glory and honor and power. For You created all things, and they exist because You created what you pleased" (Revelation 4:11).

November 28, 2006

Dear God, I love You. I am aware of Your love for me. I can see the evidence of Your love around me. I can feel Your warm, calm presence. When I pause in my daily, worldly activities to pray, to meditate, I feel a calm, peaceful sense of security take over my body. Yet, I struggle with You. I know You are wiser. I know I can trust You, intellectually. But, inwardly, I impose on myself the need to make every decision; to solve every problem; to plan my every step; as though I know best. Oh yes, I am impatient, too. I do all these things because I want to decide, plan, and get on with whatever I decide.

I have this driving principal in mind; God helps those who help themselves. I did not put that in quotes, for I believe I read somewhere that neither God not Jesus ever said it. But, knowing this intellectually has not erased that admonition from my mind. I feel obligated, as a man, to solve all my problems, make every decision, lay out all the plans with no prayer, no consultation with Jesus my Lord God.

How long does it take to change a life-long habit? What circumstances will be so desperate, so overwhelming that I will finally change? What other manly attributes can I develop to prove to myself that I am a man.? And, who must I convince I am a man?

God loves me, accepts me as I am. Isn't that enough? I will pray and meditate, seeking the Lord's guidance in all situations that confront me. I will seek the Lord repeatedly throughout the day. I will be patient! I will allow time for God's will to become apparent to me. With God's help I will change. My time here on earth is growing short. Either bodily functions will cease or Jesus' second coming could happen at any time. Today, I finally take that first step toward dependence on God to replace my misdirected "independence." God help me!

Fruit of the Spirit (9) (Galatians 5:22-23)
Fruit matures and ripens slowly. God develops the fruit of the Spirit by allowing you to experience circumstances in which you are tempted to express the exact opposite quality. God's love is everlasting and His patience endures forever.

David says, "Search me O God, and know my heart; test me and know my anxious thoughts. Point out anything in me that offends You and lead me along the path of everlasting life" (Psalm 139:23-24).

March 24, 2007

"Husbands, this means love your wives, just as Christ loved the church. He gave up His life for her" (Ephesians 5:25).

...I love my Lord Jesus: without reservations, without limits, and with respect and admiration.

March 25, 2007

Today I will visit a 9:30 a.m. class so Lyndia and I will be in the same worship service, and sing in the same choir.

March 28, 2007

"Surely Your goodness and unfailing love will pursue me all the days of my life; and I will live in the house of the LORD forever" (Psalm 23:6).

Dear Father, I delight in being in Your house. I will make my house Your house. I will create in my mind those still waters. I will praise You in my prayers and in my quiet time. I thank You for Your mercy and forgiveness. I thank You for all of the many, many blessings I have received. Amen.

April 10-2007

"No one will be able to stand against you as long as you live. For I will be with you as I was with Moses. I will not fail you or abandon you" *(Joshua 1:5).*

April 18, 2007

Yesterday was spent at St. Francis Heart Hospital. I had high expectations; I was going to be "fixed." My heart and the associated parts would be repaired and I would be made whole. I was not!

My initial reaction was disappointment and anger. I wanted to become strong again and to not become an invalid requiring Lyndia's care. I had let her down.

Today, I take what the Lord has given me. I will be positive. I will joyfully use what God has given me – no pity, no whining, no complaining. I begin this final chapter of my life with enthusiasm, looking for those places where I can be of service; where I can make a difference wherever the Lord sends me. Lyndia assures me she will be with me. Thank you Father!

Monday, April 23, 2007

"This I declare about the LORD: He alone is my refuge, my place of safety; He is my God, and I trust Him" (Psalm 91:2).

I have now, almost a week after my visit to St. Francis Heart Hospital, accepted the reality that there is no surgical "fix" for my heart and my kidneys. There is hope that the doctor will prescribe some medication strategy that may impede or slow the progress of plaque buildup in my heart and the disease in my kidneys.

I have a peace, a calm detachment from alarm, fear, or even bitterness. I am grateful for the longevity I have been granted. I am grateful for the spirit of love that permeates my family. I am grateful that my family has so quickly integrated Lyndia into the family. I have been blessed in so many ways. Jesus Christ is my greatest blessing. My family, including Nell and Lyndia are my second greatest blessings. Thank you Father, Lord God, for Your mercy, Your love, Your many wonderful blessings. I will live each day as though it is the last. Joy, peace, love, and generosity will be the hallmarks of these last days, weeks, or hopefully, years remaining. There will be no self pity. I will fight against becoming an invalid, dependent on someone else for anything, until I can no longer take care of myself. Then, I will pray for release.

April 30, 2007

Galatians 5:23b (referring to the Fruit of the Spirit) There is no law against these things!" (Note: Because the God who sent the law also sent the Spirit, the by-products of the Spirit-filled life are in perfect harmony with the intent of God's law.)

May 11, 2007

"But if He is through with me, then let Him do what seems best to Him" (2 Samuel 15:26).

Father, here I am. Modern medicine can add not one day to my life now, Father. I do not know Your will concerning my life. I don't need to know. I can only say, here I am and do as Your will dictates.

May 16, 2007

"So let us come boldly to the throne of our gracious God. There we will receive His mercy, and we will find grace to help us when we need it most" (Hebrews 4:16).

June 3, 2007

"I look up to the mountains – does my help come from there? My help comes from the LORD, who made heaven and earth. He will not let you stumble; the one who watches over you will not slumber" (Psalm 121:1-3).

I have given my life to the Lord, to be used according to His will. I ask Him to use me, guide me, and direct me; to let me use what is left of my life to the advantage of His kingdom and to His greater Glory. Amen.

July 16, 2007

"Let all that I am praise the Lord; with my whole heart, I will praise His holy name. Let all that I am praise the Lord; may I never forget the good things He does for me. He forgives all my sins and heals all my diseases. He redeems me from death and crowns me with love and tender mercies. He fills my life with good things. My youth is renewed like the eagle's!" (Psalm 103:1-5).

July 23, 2007

"Glory and honor to God forever and ever! He is the eternal King, the unseen One who never dies; He alone is God. Amen" (I Timothy 1:17).

August 6, 2007

"Your Father knows exactly what you need before you ask Him!" (Matthew 6:8).

"Then why should we ask? The point of prayer is not to get answers from God, but to have perfect oneness with Him." – *My Utmost for His Highest*, Oswald Chambers

August 28, 2007

"And you must love the Lord your God with all your heart, all your soul, and all your strength" (Deuteronomy 6:5).

Receive God's gift of Salvation and Eternal Life

"If you confess with your mouth that Jesus is Lord and believe in your heart that God raised him from the dead, you will be saved. For it is by believing in your heart that you are made right with God, and it is by confessing with your mouth that you are saved" (Romans 10:9-10).

"For everyone has sinned, we all fall short of God's glorious standard" (Romans 3:23).

"For the wages of sin is death, but the free gift of God is eternal life through Christ Jesus our Lord" (Romans 6:23).

"Jesus replied, 'I tell you the truth, unless you are born again, you cannot see the Kingdom of God'" (John 3:3).

"Jesus told him, 'I am the way, the truth, and the life. No one can come to the Father except through Me'" (John 14:6).

"He died for everyone so that those who receive His new life will no longer live for themselves. Instead they will live for Christ, who died and was raised for them" (2 Corinthians 5:15).

"This means that anyone who belongs to Christ has become a new person. The old life is gone, a new life has begun!" (2 Corinthians 5:17).

"For God loved the world so much that he gave his one and only Son, so that everyone who believes in Him will not perish but have eternal life" (John 3:16).

"Jesus told her, 'I am the resurrection and the life. Anyone who believes in Me will live, even after dying. Everyone who lives in Me and believes in Me will never ever die'" (John 11:25-26).

"Whoever has the Son has life; whoever does not have God's Son does not have life. I have written this to you who believe in the name of the Son of God, so that you may know you have eternal life" (I John 5:12-13).

9 781615 078806